★★★GRAY SPORTS ALMANAC

COMPLETE SPORTS STATISTICS
1950-2000

TABLE OF CONTENTS

AUTO RACING .... Pages: 3-20

BASEBALL .... Pages: 21-32

BASKETBALL .... Pages: 33-44

BOXING .... Pages: 45-56

FIGURE SKATING .... Pages: 57-66

FOOTBALL .... Pages: 67-74

GOLF .... Pages: 75-91

HORSE RACING .... Pages: 92-110

AUTO RACING

1950

- NASCAR Championship - Bill Rexford
- AAA Racing:
    - Henry Banks won the series championship
    - Johnnie Parsons won the Indianapolis 500
- Formula One Champion: The first World Championship for drivers under the jurisdiction of the *Fédération Internationale de l'Automobile* (FIA) is contested. The first race of the World Championship series is the British Grand Prix won by Giuseppe Farina, driving an Alfa Romeo. Farina would go on to become the first FIA World Champion.
- 24 hours of Le Mans - Louis Rosier/Jean-Louis Rosier driving a Talbot-Lago
- Rally racing:
    - M. Becquart/H. Secret won the Monte Carlo Rally driving a Hotchkiss
- Drag racing - June 19: The first commercial drag strip, the Santa Ana Drags, begins at Orange County Airport (now John Wayne Airport) in Santa Ana, in Southern California. Admission is 50 cents -- or 75 cents if the ticket holder wanted to watch the mechanics work.

1951

- NASCAR Championship - Herb Thomas
- AAA Racing:
    - Tony Bettenhausen won the series championship
    - Lee Wallard won the Indianapolis 500
- Formula One Championship - Juan Manuel Fangio of Argentina
- 24 hours of Le Mans:
    - Louis Rosier / Jean-Louis Rosier won driving a Talbot-Lago
- Rally racing:
    - Marcel Becquart / H. Secret won the Monte Carlo Rally driving a Hotchkiss
- Drag racing - NHRA founded by Wally Parks

1952

- NASCAR Championship - Tim Flock
- AAA Racing:
    - Troy Ruttman won the Indianapolis 500
    - Chuck Stevenson won the season championship
- Formula One Championship - Alberto Ascari of Italy
- 24 hours of Le Mans:
    - Hermann Lang / Fritz Reiss won, driving a Mercedes 300SL
- Rally racing:
    - Sydney Allard / George Warburton won the Monte Carlo Rally driving an Allard J2
- Drag racing - In cities and towns across North America, drag racing begins to move from the streets to organized events usually at abandoned airport strips.

AUTO RACING

1953

- NASCAR Championship - Herb Thomas
- AAA Racing:
  - Bill Vukovich won the Indianapolis 500
  - Sam Hanks won the season driving championship
- Formula One Championship - Alberto Ascari of Italy
- 24 hours of Le Mans:
  - the team of Tony Rolt / Duncan Hamilton won, driving a Jaguar C-Type
- Rally racing:
  - the team of Maurice Gatsonides / Peter Worledge won the Monte Carlo Rally driving a Ford Zephyr
- Drag racing - The NHRA held its first official race in April on a section of the Los Angeles County Fairgrounds parking lot in Pomona, California.
- World Sportscar Championship:
  - Inaugural season
  - Ferrari wins constructor's championship after 3 victories in the season.

1954

- NASCAR Championship - Lee Petty
- AAA Racing:
  - Bill Vukovich won the Indianapolis 500
  - Jimmy Bryan won the season championship
- Formula One Championship - Juan Manuel Fangio of Argentina
- 24 hours of Le Mans: the team of Froilán González / Maurice Trintignant won, driving a Ferrari 375
- Rally racing - the team of Louis Chiron / Ciro Basadonna win the Monte Carlo Rally driving a Lancia Aurelia GT
- Drag racing - The NHRA expands, sanctioning other drag strip operators in the United States
- Daytona 200 - BSA take all first five places with remainder of the team at 8th and 16th.

1955

- NASCAR Championship - Tim Flock
- AAA Racing:
  - Bob Sweikert won the Indianapolis 500
  - Bob Sweikert won the season championship
- Formula One Championship - Juan Manuel Fangio of Argentina
- 24 hours of Le Mans:
  - Pierre Levegh killed along with more than 80 spectators in the worst auto racing accident in history
  - the team of Mike Hawthorn / Ivor Bueb won, driving a Jaguar D-type
- Rally racing:
  - the team of Per Malling / Gunnar Fadum won the Monte Carlo Rally driving a Sunbeam-Talbot
- Drag racing - The NHRA staged its first "Nationals" in Great Bend, Kansas. Calvin Rice won the inaugural "Top Fuel" championship.

AUTO RACING

1956

- NASCAR Championship - Buck Baker
- The United States Auto Club (USAC) was founded to take over race sanctioning from the American Automobile Association (AAA).
- USAC Racing:
  - Pat Flaherty won the Indianapolis 500
  - Jimmy Bryan won the season championship
- Formula One Championship - Juan Manuel Fangio of Argentina
- 24 hours of Le Mans: the team of Ron Flockhart / Ninian Sanderson won, driving a Jaguar D-Type
- Rally racing:
  - the team of Ronnie Adams / Frank Biggar won the Monte Carlo Rally driving a Jaguar Mk VII
- Drag racing:
  - Art Arfons' Allison-powered "Green Monster #6" become the first member of Hot Rod Magazine's new 150-mph Club.
  - Melvin Heath won the NHRA "Top Fuel" Championship at the Nationals

1957

- NASCAR Championship - Buck Baker
- Indianapolis 500 - Sam Hanks
- USAC Racing - Jimmy Bryan won the season championship
- Formula One Championship - Juan Manuel Fangio of Argentina
- 24 hours of Le Mans:
  - the team of Ron Flockhart / Ivor Bueb won, driving a Jaguar D-Type
- Rally racing:
  - the team of Erik Carlsson / Mario Pavoni won the Finland Car Rally driving a Saab 93
- Drag racing - George Dahir won the AHRA "Top Fuel" championship at the Nationals

1958

- NASCAR Championship - Lee Petty
- Indianapolis 500 - Jimmy Bryan
- USAC Racing - Tony Bettenhausen won the season championship
- Formula One Championship - Mike Hawthorn of Great Britain
- February 23 - Cuban rebels kidnap 5-time F1 champion Juan Manuel Fangio.
- 24 hours of Le Mans: the team of Olivier Gendebien / Phil Hill won, driving a Ferrari 250TR
- Rally racing - the team of Guy Monraisse / Jacques Feret won the Monte Carlo Rally driving a Renault

AUTO RACING

1959

- Stock car racing:
    - Lee Petty won the inaugural Daytona 500
    - NASCAR Championship — Lee Petty
- Indianapolis 500 — Rodger Ward
- USAC Racing — Rodger Ward
- Formula One Champion — Jack Brabham of Australia
- 24 hours of Le Mans: Carroll Shelby / Roy Salvadori won driving an Aston Martin DBR1
- Rally racing — Paul Coltelloni / P Alexandre won the Monte Carlo Rally driving a Citroën ID
- Drag racing:
    - Chris the "Greek" Karamesines won the AHRA "Top Fuel"
    - Rodney Singer won Top Eliminator at the NHRA Nationals

1960

- Stock car racing:
    - Junior Johnson won the Daytona 500
    - NASCAR Championship - Rex White
- Indianapolis 500 - Jim Rathmann
- USAC Racing - A.J. Foyt won the season championship
- Formula One Championship - Jack Brabham of Australia
- 24 hours of Le Mans: the team of Olivier Gendebien / Paul Frère won, driving a Ferrari TR60
- Rally racing - the team of Walter Schock / Rolf Moll won the Monte Carlo Rally driving a Mercedes 220SE.
- Drag racing - Leonard Harris won "Top Eliminator" at the NHRA Nationals

1961

- Stock car racing:
    - Marvin Panch won the Daytona 500
    - NASCAR Championship - Ned Jarrett
- Indianapolis 500 - A.J. Foyt
- USAC Racing - A.J. Foyt won the driving championship
- Formula One Championship - Phil Hill of the United States
- 24 hours of Le Mans: the team of Olivier Gendebien / Phil Hill win, driving a Ferrari TR61
- Rally racing - the team of Maurice Martin / Roger Bateau won the Monte Carlo Rally driving a Panhard PL17
- Drag racing - Pete Robinson won Top Eliminator at the NHRA Nationals

AUTO RACING

1962

- Stock car racing:
    - Fireball Roberts won the Daytona 500
    - NASCAR Championship - Joe Weatherly
- Indianapolis 500 - Rodger Ward
- USAC Racing - Rodger Ward won the season championship
- Formula One Championship - Graham Hill of Great Britain
- 24 hours of Le Mans: won by the team of Olivier Gendebien / Phil Hill driving a Ferrari 330LM
- Rally racing - the team of Erik Carlsson / Gunnar Haggbom won the Monte Carlo Rally driving a Saab 96
- Drag racing - Jack Chrisman won Top Eliminator at the NHRA Nationals

1963

- Stock car racing:
    - Tiny Lund won the Daytona 500
    - NASCAR Championship - Joe Weatherly
- Indianapolis 500 - Parnelli Jones
- USAC Racing - A.J. Foyt won the season championship
- Formula One Championship - Jimmy Clark of Great Britain
- 24 hours of Le Mans: the team of Ludovico Scarfiotti / Lorenzo Bandini win, driving a Ferrari 250P
- Rally racing - the team of Erik Carlsson / Gunnar Palm win the Monte Carlo Rally driving a Saab 96
- Drag racing - Bobby Vodnik won "Top Fuel" at the NHRA Nationals

1964

- Stock car racing:
    - Richard Petty won the Daytona 400 on February 23
    - NASCAR Championship - Richard Petty
- Indianapolis 500 - A.J. Foyt
- USAC Racing - A.J. Foyt won the season championship
- Formula One Championship - John Surtees of Great Britain
- 24 hours of Le Mans: the team of Jean Guichet / Nino Vaccarella won driving a Ferrari 275P
- Rally racing - the team of Paddy Hopkirk / Henry Liddon won the Monte Carlo Rally driving a Mini Cooper S
- Drag racing - Don Garlits won the NHRA, Top Fuel Championship

AUTO RACING

1968

- Stock car racing:
    - Cale Yarborough won the Daytona 500
    - NASCAR Championship - David Pearson
- Indianapolis 500 - Bobby Unser
- USAC Racing - Bobby Unser won the season championship
- Formula One Champion: Graham Hill of Great Britain
- 24 hours of Le Mans: the team of Pedro Rodriguez / Lucien Bianchi won driving a Ford GT-40
- Rally racing - Vic Elford / David Stone won the Monte Carlo Rally driving a Porsche 911T
- Drag racing - Don Garlits won the NHRA "Top Fuel" Championship

1969

- Stock car racing:
    - LeeRoy Yarbrough won the Daytona 500
    - NASCAR Championship - David Pearson
- Indianapolis 500 - Mario Andretti
- USAC Racing - Mario Andretti won the season championship
- Formula One Championship - Jackie Stewart of Great Britain driving a Matra
- 24 hours of Le Mans:
    - Jacky Ickx / Jackie Oliver won driving a Ford GT-40
- Rally racing - the team of Bjorn Waldegard / Lars Helmer won the Monte Carlo Rally driving a Porsche 911S
- Drag racing:
    - Don Prudhomme won the NHRA's "Top Fuel" championship
    - Steve Carbone won "Top Fuel" at the NHRA World Finals

1970

- Stock car racing:
    - Pete Hamilton won the Daytona 500
    - NASCAR Championship - Bobby Isaac
- Indianapolis 500 - Al Unser, Sr.
- USAC Racing - Al Unser, Sr. won the season championship
- Formula One Championship - Jochen Rindt of Austria)becomes Formula One's only posthumous world champion
- 24 hours of Le Mans: the team of Hans Herrmann / Richard Attwood won, driving a Porsche 917
- Rally racing - the team of Bjorn Waldegard / Lars Helmer won the Monte Carlo Rally driving a Porsche 911S.
- Drag racing - the NHRA launches the "Supernationals". Rick Ramsey wins "Top Fuel"

AUTO RACING

1971

- Stock car racing:
    - Richard Petty won the Daytona 500
    - NASCAR Championship - Richard Petty
- Indianapolis 500 - Al Unser, Sr
- USAC Racing - Joe Leonard
- Formula One Championship - Jackie Stewart of Great Britain
- 24 hours of Le Mans: the team of Helmut Marko / Gijs van Lennep won, driving a Porsche 917
- Rally racing - the team of Ove Andersson / David Stone won the Monte Carlo Rally driving an Alpine-Renault A110
- Drag racing:
    - The NHRA announces the first "Grandnational" in Canada at Sanair International Drag Strip, near Montreal, Quebec.
    - Hank Johnson won Top Fuel at the NHRA Supernationals.

1972

- Stock car racing:
    - February 20: A.J. Foyt won the Daytona 500
    - NASCAR Championship - Richard Petty
- Indianapolis 500 - Mark Donohue
- USAC Racing - Joe Leonard won the season championship
- Formula 5000 - Gijs van Lennep of The Netherlands
- Formula One Championship - Emerson Fittipaldi of Brazil
- 24 hours of Le Mans: the team of Henri Pescarolo / Graham Hill won, driving a Matra MS670
- Rally racing - Sandro Munari / Mario Manucci won the Monte Carlo Rally driving a Lancia Fulvia 1.6HF
- Drag racing - Don Moody won "Top Fuel" at the NHRA Supernationals

1973

- Stock car racing:
    - Richard Petty wins the Daytona 500 in which singer Marty Robbins made his first appearance as a driver.
    - NASCAR Championship - Benny Parsons
- Indianapolis 500 - Gordon Johncock
- USAC Racing - Roger McCluskey
- Formula One Championship - Jackie Stewart of Great Britain
- 24 hours of Le Mans: the team of Henri Pescarolo / Gérard Larrousse won, driving a Matra MS670B
- Rally racing - Jean-Claude Andruet / Michele Petit ("Biche") won the Monte Carlo Rally driving a Alpine-Renault A110. This year's rally was the first ever Fédération Internationale de l'Automobile World Rally Championship event.
- Drag racing - Don Garlits won "Top Fuel" at the NHRA Supernationals

AUTO RACING

1974

- Stock car racing:
    - Richard Petty won the Daytona 500
    - NASCAR Championship - Richard Petty
    - IROC Championship - inaugural year won by Mark Donohue
- Indianapolis 500 - Johnny Rutherford
- USAC Racing - Bobby Unser
- Formula One Championship - Emerson Fittipaldi of Brazil
- 24 hours of Le Mans: the team of Henri Pescarolo / Gérard Larrousse won, driving a Matra MS670B
- Rally racing - In the first rally to cross the Sahara Desert, the Australian team of Ken Tubman, Andre Welenski, and Jim Reddiex won the "World Cup Rally" driving a Citroën.
- Drag racing - Don Garlits won "Top Fuel" at the NHRA World Finals

1975

- Stock car racing:
    - Benny Parsons won the Daytona 500
    - NASCAR Championship - Richard Petty
- Indianapolis 500 - Bobby Unser
- USAC Racing - A.J. Foyt won the season championship
- Formula One Championship - Niki Lauda of Austria
- 24 hours of Le Mans:
    - the team of Jacky Ickx / Derek Bell won, driving a Mirage GR8
- Rally racing - the team of Sandro Munari / Mario Manucci won the Monte Carlo Rally driving a Lancia Stratos HF
- Drag racing - Don Garlits won the NHRA "Top Fuel" championship.

1976

- Stock car racing:
    - February 15 David Pearson won the Daytona 500
    - NASCAR Championship - Cale Yarborough
- Indianapolis 500 - Johnny Rutherford
- USAC Racing - Gordon Johncock won the season championship
- Formula One Championship:
    - James Hunt of Britain
    - Niki Lauda's famous accident occurred during the German Grand Prix at Nürburgring
- 24 hours of Le Mans: the team of Jacky Ickx / Gijs van Lennep won, driving a Porsche 936
- Rally racing - the team of Sandro Munari / Mario Manucci won the Monte Carlo Rally driving a Lancia Stratos HF
- Drag racing: Shirley Muldowney won "Top Fuel" at the NHRA World Finals
- Touring car racing: Bob Morris and John Fitzpatrick won the Bathurst 1000, driving a Holden Torana

AUTO RACING

1977

- Stock car racing:
    - NASCAR Championship - Cale Yarborough
    - Cale Yarborough won the Daytona 500
- USAC Racing - Tom Sneva wins the season championship
    - Indianapolis 500 - won by A.J. Foyt. Janet Guthrie became first female qualifier
- Formula One Champion - Niki Lauda of Austria
- 24 hours of Le Mans: the team of Jean-Pierre Laussaud / Didier Pironi won, driving a Renault-Alpine 442
- Rally racing:
    - The team of Sandro Munari / Silvio Maiga won the Monte Carlo Rally driving a Lancia Stratos HF
    - Andrew Cowan won the Singapore Airlines London to Sydney Rally driving a Mercedes
- Drag racing:
    - Shirley Muldowney won the NHRA Top Fuel championship.
    - Dennis Baca won Top Fuel at the NHRA World Finals
- Touring car racing: Allan Moffat and Jacky Ickx won the Bathurst 1000, driving a Ford Falcon

1978

- Stock car racing: NASCAR Championship - Cale Yarborough
- USAC - A J Foyt won final season championship under USAC.
    - CART, Championship Auto Racing Teams open wheel racing established in the United States.
    - Indianapolis 500 - won by Al Unser Snr
- Touring car racing: Peter Brock and Jim Richards won the Bathurst 1000, driving a Holden Torana

1979

- Stock car racing:
    - NASCAR Championship - Richard Petty
    - February - Richard Petty won the Daytona 500
- CART Racing (replaced USAC): Rick Mears won the season championship
    - May - Indianapolis 500 - Rick Mears
- Formula One Champion - Jody Scheckter of South Africa
- 24 hours of Le Mans: the team of Klaus Ludwig / Bill Whittington / Don Whittington win driving a Porsche 935
- Rally racing - the team of Bernard Darniche / Alain Mahe win the Monte Carlo Rally driving a Lancia Stratos HF
- Drag racing:
    - Rob Bruins won the NHRA Top Fuel championship.
    - Don Garlits won Top Fuel at the [NHRA] World Finals
- Touring car racing - Peter Brock and Jim Richards won their second consecutive Bathurst 1000, driving a Holden Torana

AUTO RACING

1980

- Stock car racing:
    - NASCAR Championship - Dale Earnhardt
    - Buddy Baker won the Daytona 500
- CART Racing - Johnny Rutherford won the season championship
    - Indianapolis 500 - Johnny Rutherford
- Formula One Champion - Alan Jones of Australia
- 24 hours of Le Mans: the team of Jean Rondeau / Jean-Pierre Jaussaud won, driving a Rondeau M379B
- Rally racing - Walter Röhrl in a Fiat won the World Rally Championship
    - The team of Walter Röhrl / Christian Geistdorfer won the Monte Carlo Rally driving a Fiat 131 Abarth
- Drag racing - Shirley Muldowney won the NHRA Top Fuel championship.
- Touring car racing - Peter Brock and Jim Richards won their third consecutive Bathurst 1000, driving a Holden Torana

1981

- Stock car racing:
    - NASCAR Championship - Darrell Waltrip
    - Richard Petty won the Daytona 500
- CART Racing - Rick Mears won the season championship
    - May 25 - Indianapolis 500 - Bobby Unser
- Formula One Champion - Nelson Piquet of Brazil
- 24 hours of Le Mans:
    - teammates Jacky Ickx / Derek Bell won, driving a Porsche 936
- Rally racing - Ari Vatanen in a Ford won the World Rally Championship
    - the team of Jean Ragnotti / Jean-Marc Andrie won the Monte Carlo Rally driving a Renault 5 Turbo
- Drag racing: Gary Beck won "Top Fuel" at the NHRA World Finals

1982

- Stock car racing:
    - NASCAR Championship - Darrell Waltrip
    - Bobby Allison won the Daytona 500
- CART Racing - Rick Mears won the season championship
    - Indianapolis 500 - Gordon Johncock
- Formula One Champion - Keke Rosberg of Finland
- 24 hours of Le Mans:
    - won by the team of Jacky Ickx / Derek Bell driving a Porsche 956
- Rally racing - Walter Röhrl in an Opel won the World Rally Championship
    - Walter Rohrl / Christian Geistdorfer won the Monte Carlo Rally driving an Opel Ascona 400
- Drag racing - Shirley Muldowney won the NHRA Top Fuel championship.

AUTO RACING

1983

- Stock car racing:
    - NASCAR Championship - Bobby Allison
    - Cale Yarborough won the Daytona 500
- CART Racing - Al Unser won the season championship
    - Indianapolis 500 - Tom Sneva
- Formula One Championship - Nelson Piquet of Brazil
- 24 hours of Le Mans: the team of Vern Schuppan / Al Holbert / Hurley Haywood won, driving a Porsche 956
- Rally racing - Hannu Mikkola in an Audi won the World Rally Championship
    - the team of Walter Röhrl / Christian Geistdorfer won the Monte Carlo Rally driving a Lancia 037
- Drag racing - Gary Beck won the NHRA Top Fuel championship.

1984

- Stock car racing:
    - NASCAR Championship - Terry Labonte
    - Cale Yarborough won the Daytona 500
    - Richard Petty won the 200th (and final) race of his career on July 4.
- CART Racing - Mario Andretti won the season championship
    - Indianapolis 500 - Rick Mears
- Formula One Championship - Niki Lauda of Austria
- 24 hours of Le Mans:
    - the team of Klaus Ludwig / Henri Pescarolo won, driving a Porsche 956
- Rally racing - Stig Blomqvist in an Audi won the World Rally Championship
    - the team of Walter Röhrl / Christian Geistdorfer won the Monte Carlo Rally driving an Audi Quattro
- Drag racing - Joe Amato won the NHRA Top Fuel championship.

1985

- Stock car racing:
    - Bill Elliott won the Daytona 500
    - NASCAR Championship - Darrell Waltrip
    - Ken Schrader enters NASCAR
- CART Racing - Al Unser Sr won the season championship
    - Indianapolis 500 - Danny Sullivan
- Formula One Championship - Alain Prost of France
- 24 hours of Le Mans: the team of Klaus Ludwig / Paolo Barilla / "John Winter" (Louis Krages) won, driving a Porsche 956
- Rally racing - Timo Salonen in a Peugeot won the World Rally Championship
    - the team of Ari Vatanen / Terry Harryman won the Monte Carlo Rally driving a Peugeot 205T16
- Drag racing:
    - Don Garlits won the NHRA Top Fuel championship
    - Gary Beck won Top Fuel at the NHRA World Finals

AUTO RACING

1986

- Stock car racing:
  - February - Geoff Bodine won the Daytona 500
  - NASCAR Championship - Dale Earnhardt
- CART Racing - Bobby Rahal
  - June - Indianapolis 500 - Bobby Rahal Note: this race was run on a Saturday 6 days after the race was rained out.
- Formula One Championship - Alain Prost of France
- 24 hours of Le Mans: the team of Derek Bell / Hans-Joachim Stuck / Al Holbert won, driving a Porsche 962C
- Rally racing - Juha Kankkunen in a Peugeot won the World Rally Championship
  - the team of Henri Toivonen / Sergio Cresto won the Monte Carlo Rally driving a Lancia Delta S4
- Drag racing:
  - Don Garlits won the NHRA "Top Fuel" championship
  - Darrell Gwynn won Top Fuel at the NHRA Winston Finals

1987

- Stock car racing:
  - Bill Elliott won the Daytona 500
  - NASCAR Championship - Dale Earnhardt
- CART Racing - Bobby Rahal won the season championship
  - Indianapolis 500 - Al Unser, Sr.
- Formula One Championship - Nelson Piquet of Brazil
- 24 hours of Le Mans: won by the team of Derek Bell / Hans-Joachim Stuck / Al Holbert driving a Porsche 962C
- Rally racing - Juha Kankkunen in a Lancia won the World Rally Championship
  - the team of Miki Biasion / Tiziano Siviero won the Monte Carlo Rally driving a Lancia Delta HF 4x4
- Drag racing:
  - Dick LaHaie won the NHRA "Top Fuel" championship
  - Darrell Gwynn won Top Fuel at the NHRA Winston Finals

1988

- Stock car racing:
  - Bobby Allison won the Daytona 500
  - NASCAR Championship - Bill Elliott
- CART Racing - Danny Sullivan won the season championship
  - Indianapolis 500 - Rick Mears
- Formula One Championship - Ayrton Senna of Brazil
- 24 hours of Le Mans:
  - won by the team of Jan Lammers / Johnny Dumfries / Andy Wallace driving a Jaguar XJR-9LM
- Rally racing - Miki Biasion in a Lancia won the World Rally Championship
  - the team of Bruno Saby / Jean-Francois Fauchille won the Monte Carlo Rally driving a Lancia Delta HF 4x4
- Drag racing - Joe Amato won the NHRA "Top Fuel" championship.

AUTO RACING

1989

- Stock car racing:
    - Darrell Waltrip won the Daytona 500
    - NASCAR Championship - Rusty Wallace
- CART Racing - season championship won by Emerson Fittipaldi
    - Indianapolis 500 - Emerson Fittipaldi
- Formula One Championship - Alain Prost of France
- 24 hours of Le Mans:
    - won by the team of Jochen Mass / Manuel Reuter / Stanley Dickens driving a Sauber-Mercedes
- Rally racing - Miki Biasion in a Lancia won the World Rally Championship
    - the team of Miki Biasion / Tiziano Siviero won the Monte Carlo Rally driving a Lancia Delta HF Integrale
- Drag racing - Gary Ormsby won the NHRA "Top Fuel" championship.

1990

- Stock car racing:
    - Derrike Cope won the Daytona 500
    - NASCAR Championship - Dale Earnhardt
- CART Racing - Al Unser, Jr. won the season championship
    - Indianapolis 500 - Arie Luyendyk of The Netherlands
- Formula One Championship - Ayrton Senna of Brazil
- 24 hours of Le Mans:
    - won by the team of John Nielsen / Price Cobb / Martin Brundle driving a Jaguar XJR-12.
- Rally racing - Carlos Sainz in a Toyota won the World Rally Championship
    - the team of Didier Auriol/Bernard Occelli won the Monte Carlo Rally driving a Lancia Delta HF Integrale
- Drag racing - Joe Amato won the NHRA "Top Fuel" championship.

1991

- Stock car racing:
    - Ernie Irvan won the Daytona 500
    - NASCAR Championship - Dale Earnhardt
- CART Racing - Michael Andretti won the season championship
    - Indianapolis 500 - Rick Mears
- Formula One Championship - Ayrton Senna of Brazil
- 24 hours of Le Mans: won by Volker Weidler / Johnny Herbert / Bertrand Gachot driving a Mazda 787
- Rally racing - Juha Kankkunen in a Lancia won the World Rally Championship
    - the team of Carlos Sainz / Luis Moya won the Monte Carlo Rally driving a Toyota Celica GT4
- Drag racing - Joe Amato won the NHRA "Top Fuel" championship.

AUTO RACING

1992

- Stock car racing:
    - Davey Allison won the Daytona 500
    - NASCAR Championship - Alan Kulwicki
- CART Racing - season championship won by Bobby Rahal
    - Indianapolis 500 - Al Unser, Jr.
- Formula One Championship:
    - Nigel Mansell of Great Britain
    - Giovanna Amati the last women to appear on the entry list for a Formula One Grand Prix to date.
- 24 hours of Le Mans: the team of Derek Warwick / Yannick Dalmas / Mark Blundell won, driving a Peugeot 905
- Rally racing - Carlos Sainz in a Toyota Celica won the World Rally Championship
    - the team of Didier Auriol / Bernard Occelli won the Monte Carlo Rally driving a Lancia Delta Integrale HF
- Drag racing - Joe Amato won the NHRA "Top Fuel" championship.

1993

- Stock car racing:
    - Dale Jarrett won the Daytona 500
    - NASCAR Championship - Dale Earnhardt
    - Two top NASCAR drivers--Alan Kulwicki, the 1992 series champion, and Davey Allison, were killed in aviation accidents. Kulwicki died in a plane crash on his way to a race; Allison died from injuries suffered in a helicopter crash during a race weekend.
- CART Racing - season championship won by Nigel Mansell
    - Indianapolis 500 - Emerson Fittipaldi
- Formula One Championship - Alain Prost of France (Williams-Renault)
- 24 hours of Le Mans:
    - won by the team of Geoff Brabham / Christophe Bouchut / Éric Helary driving a Peugeot 905
- Rally racing - Juha Kankkunen won the World Rally Championship in a Toyota
    - the team of Didier Auriol / Bernard Occelli won the Monte Carlo Rally driving a Toyota Celica Turbo 4WD
- Drag racing:
    - Eddie Hill won the NHRA "Top Fuel" championship
    - Rance McDaniel won Top Fuel at the NHRA Winston Finals

AUTO RACING

1994

- Stock car racing:
  - Sterling Marlin won the Daytona 500
  - NASCAR Championship - Dale Earnhardt
- CART Racing - season championship won by Al Unser, Jr.
  - Indianapolis 500 - Al Unser, Jr.
- Formula One - Michael Schumacher wins the Drivers' Championship.
  - The season is marred when, during qualifying for the San Marino Grand Prix, Roland Ratzenberger crashes at the Villeneuve corner and dies from his injuries. The race goes ahead and Ayrton Senna crashes at Tamburello and dies as well.
- 24 hours of Le Mans: Yannick Dalmas / Hurley Haywood / Mauro Baldi won, driving a Porsche 962LM
- Rally racing - Didier Auriol won the World Rally Championship
  - the team of François Delecour / Daniel Grataloup won the Monte Carlo Rally driving a Ford Escort RS Cosworth
- Drag racing - Scott Kalitta won the NHRA "Top Fuel" championship.

1995

- Stock car racing:
  - Sterling Marlin won the Daytona 500
  - NASCAR Championship - Jeff Gordon
- CART racing - season championship won by Jacques Villeneuve
  - Indianapolis 500 - Jacques Villeneuve. (First IRL races following year).
- Formula One Championship - Michael Schumacher of Germany
- 24 hours of Le Mans: Yannick Dalmas / J.J. Lehto / Masanori Sekiya won, driving a McLaren F1-GTR
- Rally racing - Colin McRae won the World Rally Championship
  - Carlos Sainz /Luis Moya won the Monte Carlo Rally driving a Subaru Impreza 555
- Drag racing - Scott Kalitta won the NHRA "Top Fuel" championship.

1996

- Stock car racing:
  - Dale Jarrett won the Daytona 500
- NASCAR Championship - Terry Labonte
  - Rusty Wallace wins the Suzuka NASCAR Thunder 100 at Suzuka City November 24, the first NASCAR event held in Japan.
- Indy Racing League - Scott Sharp and Buzz Calkins tie for the inaugural IRL championship
  - Indianapolis 500 - Buddy Lazier
- CART - Jimmy Vasser won the season championship
- Formula One Championship - Damon Hill of Great Britain
- 24 hours of Le Mans: won by the team of Manuel Reuter / Davy Jones / Alexander Wurz driving a TWR-Porsche
- Rally racing - Tommi Mäkinen won the World Rally Championship
  - the team of Patrick Bernardini / Bernard Occelli won the Monte Carlo Rally
- Drag racing - Kenny Bernstein won the NHRA "Top Fuel" championship.

AUTO RACING

1997

- Stock car racing:
    - Jeff Gordon is the youngest driver ever to win the Daytona 500 on February 16
    - NASCAR Championship - Jeff Gordon
- Indy Racing League -
- Indianapolis 500 - Arie Luyendyk of The Netherlands
- CART Racing - Alex Zanardi won the season championship
- Formula One Championship - Jacques Villeneuve of Canada
- V8 Supercars Australia
    - Championship Series won by Glenn Seton in a Ford Falcon EL.
    - Bathurst 1000 for V8 Supercars won by Russel Ingall and Larry Perkins in a Holden Commodore VS.
    - Bathurst 1000 for Super Touring won by Jim Richards and Rickard Rydell. Rydell setting a shootout lap of 2:14.x. fastest super touring lap ever around the mountain at that time.
- 24 hours of Le Mans: the team of Michele Alboreto / Stefan Johansson / Tom Kristensen won, driving a TWR-Porsche
- Rally racing - Tommi Mäkinen won the World Rally Championship
    - the team of Piero Liatti / Fabrizia Pons won the Monte Carlo Rally driving a Subaru Impreza WRC97
- Drag racing - Gary Scelzi won the NHRA "Top Fuel" championship.

1998

- Stock car racing:
    - Dale Earnhardt won the Daytona 500
    - NASCAR Championship - Jeff Gordon
    - NASCAR celebrates its 50th anniversary
- Indy Racing League -
- Indianapolis 500 - Eddie Cheever
- CART Racing - Alex Zanardi won the season championship
- Formula One Championship - Mika Häkkinen of Finland
- 24 hours of Le Mans: won by the team of Laurent Aïello / Allan McNish / Stéphane Ortelli driving a Porsche 911 GT-1
- Rally racing - Tommi Mäkinen won the World Rally Championship
    - the team of Carlos Sainz / Luis Moya won the Monte Carlo Rally driving a Toyota Corolla WRC
- Drag racing - Gary Scelzi won the NHRA "Top Fuel" championship.

AUTO RACING

1999

- Stock car racing:
    - Jeff Gordon won the Daytona 500
    - NASCAR Championship - Dale Jarrett
- Indy Racing League -
- Indianapolis 500 - Kenny Bräck
- CART Racing - Juan Pablo Montoya won the season championship
- Formula One Championship - Mika Häkkinen of Finland
- 24 hours of Le Mans: won by the team of Pierluigi Martini / Yannick Dalmas / Joachim Winkelhock driving a BMW V-12 LMR
- World Rally Championship - Tommi Mäkinen / Risto Mannisenmäki of Finland
- Drag racing - Tony Schumacher won the NHRA "Top Fuel" championship.
- Formula Nippon - Tom Coronel of The Netherlands.

2000

- Stock car racing:
    - Dale Jarrett won the Daytona 500
    - NASCAR Championship - Bobby Labonte
    - Adam Petty, Kenny Irwin, Jr., Scott Baker, and Tony Roper all died from head-related injuries that brought safety concerns to NASCAR
    - February 20 - The 2000 NASCAR Winston Cup Series Daytona 500 Winner=Dale Jarrett
    - February 27 - The 2000 NASCAR Winston Cup Series Dura-Lube/Kmart 400 at North Carolina Motor Speedway Winner=Bobby Labonte
- Indy Racing League - Buddy Lazier won the season championship
- Indianapolis 500 - Juan Pablo Montoya
- CART Racing - Gil de Ferran won the season championship
- Formula One Championship - Michael Schumacher of Germany
- 24 hours of Le Mans: Frank Biela / Tom Kristensen / Emanuele Pirro won, driving an (Audi R8R LMP)
- World Rally Championship - Marcus Grönholm of Finland
- Drag racing - Gary Scelzi won the NHRA "Top Fuel" championship.

BASEBALL

1950

- World Series: New York Yankees win 4 games to 0 over the Philadelphia Phillies

1951

- January 26: Mel Ott and Jimmie Foxx are inducted into the Baseball Hall of Fame.
- January 29: Baseball signs a six-year All-Star game pact for TV-radio rights for $6 million. A number of owners criticize lame-duck Commissioner Happy Chandler, believing that in a couple of years, the broadcast rights would be worth much more than $1 million per annum.
- April 17: Mickey Mantle makes his Major League debut.
- May 7: Johnny Vander Meer pitches in his final Major League game.
- May 25: The New York Giants rookie Willie Mays, goes 0-for-5 in his major league debut against the Philadelphia Phillies.
- July 10: Alfonso "Chico" Carrasquel became the first Latin American player to participate in an All-Star game, beating out reigning MVP Phil Rizzuto as the American League's starting shortstop. Carrasquel would go on to be selected to the All-Star team a total of four times.
- July 14 - St. Louis Browns sign Satchel Paige as a free agent.
- August 11: The New York Giants fall 13 games behind in the National League standings. Following this nadir, the Giants go 37-8 over their last 45 games in one of baseball's most famous comebacks. This enables them to tie their crosstown rivals Brooklyn Dodgers for first place and forces a playoff series.
- August 19: 3' 7" Eddie Gaedel becomes the only midget to play in a major league game, pinch-hitting and drawing a walk in his lone plate appearance.
- August 29 - The New York Yankees trade Lew Burdette and $50,000 cash to the Boston Braves for Johnny Sain.
- September 7 - Bobby Doerr plays in his final career game.
- September 30 - Joe DiMaggio plays in his final career regular season game.
- October 4: National League Playoff: The New York Giants and the Brooklyn Dodgers finished the season tied for first place. The Giants then won a playoff series, 2 games to 1. In the final game, when all seemed lost for the Giants, Bobby Thomson hit a dramatic three run homer in the bottom of the ninth inning to give the Giants a 5 to 4 victory and the National League pennant.
- World Series: New York Yankees win 4 games to 2 over the New York Giants
- MVP Awards: Roy Campanella (NL) and Yogi Berra (AL)
- Rookie of the Year Awards: Willie Mays (NL) and Gil McDougald (AL)
- Babe Ruth Award: Phil Rizzuto
- Sporting News Major League Player of the Year: Stan Musial
- Sporting News Pitcher of the Year: Preacher Roe (NL) and Bob Feller (AL)

1952

- January 31: The Hall of Fame elects two new members: Harry Heilmann, with 203 votes, and Paul Waner with 195. Waner, a .333 career hitter, rapped out 3,152 hits and struck out just 376 times in 9,459 career at-bats. Heilmann was similarly skilled with the bat, winning four batting titles with the Tigers and finishing his career with a .342 average
- World Series: New York Yankees win 4 games to 3 over the Brooklyn Dodgers

BASEBALL

1953

- World Series: New York Yankees won 4 games to 2 over the Brooklyn Dodgers

1954

- January 14: Former Yankees great Joe DiMaggio marries legendary actress Marilyn Monroe in a union of heavily publicized media stars.
- World Series: New York Giants win 4 games to 0 over the Cleveland Indians

1955

- April 23: The White Sox tallied a franchise record 29 runs at Kansas City. Sherm Lollar was 5-for-6 with a pair of home runs and five RBI, while reserve outfielder Bob Nieman and infielder Walt Dropo drove in seven runs apiece, and Chico Carrasquel hit 5-for-6 with five runs, in the 29-6 victory over the Athletics.
- World Series: October 4 - Brooklyn Dodgers win 4 games to 3 over the New York Yankees. The Series MVP is pitcher Johnny Podres, Brooklyn.

1956

- April 17: Luis Aparicio replaces fellow Venezuelan Chico Carrasquel as the White Sox' everyday shortstop. Aparicio, who played 10 seasons with the White Sox, was elected to the Hall of Fame in 1984 and had his #11 retired by the Sox in the same year.
- July 14: Boston Red Sox lefty Mel Parnell pitches a no-hitter against the Chicago White Sox at Fenway Park, winning 4-0. It is only Parnell's third win against two losses and is the sixth straight loss for second-place Chicago. The no-hitter is the first for the Red Sox since 1923. Parnell will go 4-4 before a torn muscle in his pitching arm ends his career as the Red Sox' winningest southpaw.
- World Series: New York Yankees win 4 games to 3 over the Brooklyn Dodgers. Yankees pitcher Don Larsen, pitches the first and only perfect game in World Series history, earning himself MVP honors. It is also the only no-hitter thrown in any postseason game.
- December 1: Cincinnati slugger Frank Robinson is unanimously voted the NL Rookie of the Year. White Sox shortstop Luis Aparicio is voted AL Rookie of the Year with 22 points, beating out Baltimore's Tito Francona and Rocky Colavito of the Indians.

BASEBALL

1957

- January 5 - Jackie Robinson retires rather than move across town from the Dodgers to the Giants, to whom he had been traded in December.
- Roy Sievers lead American league with 42 home runs and 114 RBIs, for the last place Washington Senators.
- Cy Young Award: Warren Spahn, Milwaukee Braves
- World Series: Milwaukee Braves defeat New York Yankees four games to three.
- May 3 - Walter O'Malley, the owner of the Brooklyn Dodgers, agrees to move the team from Brooklyn, New York, to Los Angeles, California.
- August 19- Horace Stoneham announces that the Giants are moving from New York to San Francisco, California.
- October 8 - Walter O'Malley announces that the Dodgers are going to move from Brooklyn, New York to Los Angeles, California.
- The Winnipeg Goldeyes win the Northern League championship.

1958

- January 29: The Brooklyn Dodgers catcher Roy Campanella suffers a broken neck in an early morning auto accident on Long Island. His spinal column is nearly severed and his legs are permanently paralyzed.
- January 30: Commissioner Ford Frick announces that players and coaches, rather than the fans, will vote for the All-Star teams.
- April 15: San Francisco Giants pitcher Rubén Gómez won baseball's first regular season game on the West Coast. He started the first game in San Francisco history, beating Don Drysdale and the visiting Los Angeles Dodgers in an 8-0 shutout at Seals Stadium. The two teams moved from New York after the 1957 season.
- World Series: New York Yankees win 4 games to 3 over the Milwaukee Braves. The Series MVP is pitcher Bob Turley of New York.

1959

- March 3 — The San Francisco Giants officially name their new stadium Candlestick Park.
- World Series: Los Angeles Dodgers win 4 games to 2 over the Chicago White Sox. The Series MVP is Larry Sherry, Los Angeles
- The Winnipeg Goldeyes win the Northern League championship.

1960

- World Series: Pittsburgh Pirates win 4 games to 3 over the New York Yankees. The Series MVP is Bobby Richardson, New York.
- October 13 - 1960 World Series: Baseballer Bill Mazeroski becomes the first person to end a World Series with a home run.
- The Winnipeg Goldeyes win the Northern League championship.

BASEBALL

1961

- January 16: Mickey Mantle becomes the highest paid player in Major League Baseball by signing a contract that will pay him $75,000 per season.
- April 11: The former Washington Senators play their first home game in Metropolitan Stadium as the Minnesota Twins.
- July 13: In his majors debut, Milwaukee Braves outfielder Mack Jones tied a post-1900 National League record by collecting three singles and a double in his first game.
- Roger Maris hits 61 home runs during the regular season, breaking Babe Ruth's mark of 60 that had stood since 1927.
- October - World Series: New York Yankees win 4 games to 1 over the Cincinnati Reds. The series MVP is Whitey Ford of the Yankees.

1962

- January 23: Bob Feller and Jackie Robinson are selected for the Baseball Hall of Fame in their first years of eligibility.
- October: National League pennant playoff: After finishing tied for the league lead, the Los Angeles Dodgers and San Francisco Giants played-off for the title. The Giants won the series 2 games to 1, thereby winning the National League championship.
- World Series: New York Yankees win 4 games to 3 over the San Francisco Giants. The Series MVP was Ralph Terry, New York.

1963

- June 22: Phillies center fielder Tony Gonzalez plays his 200th straight errorless game to help rookie Ray Culp beat Roger Craig and the Mets 2-0.
- World Series: Los Angeles Dodgers win 4 games to 0 over the New York Yankees. The series MVP is Sandy Koufax, Los Angeles.

1964

- World Series: St. Louis Cardinals win 4 games to 3 over the New York Yankees. The Series MVP is pitcher, Bob Gibson of St. Louis.

1965

- World Series: Los Angeles Dodgers win 4 games to 3 over the Minnesota Twins. The Series MVP was Sandy Koufax, Los Angeles.

BASEBALL

1966

- January 20: The BBWAA elects Ted Williams to the Hall of Fame. Williams, the last batter to hit .400, receives 282 of a possible 302 votes.
- Roberto Clemente is the National League MVP.
- Frank Robinson is the American League MVP.
- Ted Williams is inducted into Baseball Hall of Fame.
- World Series: Baltimore Orioles win 4 games to 0 over the Los Angeles Dodgers. Series MVP: Frank Robinson, Baltimore.

1967

- World Series: St. Louis Cardinals win 4 games to 3 over the Boston Red Sox. The series MVP is pitcher Bob Gibson of St. Louis.

1968

- January 23: Joe Medwick is voted into the Baseball Hall of Fame. Medwick won the Triple Crown in 1937 and batted .300 in 14 of 17 seasons.
- January 28: Goose Goslin and Kiki Cuyler are admitted to the Hall of Fame by unanimous vote of the Special Veterans Committee. Goslin was a career .316 hitter who played in four World Series. Cuyler was a .321 career hitter with four stolen base crowns.
- Denny McLain of the Detroit Tigers becomes the first pitcher in Major League Baseball to win 30 or more games since Dizzy Dean of the St. Louis Cardinals in 1934. Since McLain, no pitcher has accomplished that feat.
- World Series: Detroit Tigers won 4 games to 3 over the St. Louis Cardinals. The Series MVP was Mickey Lolich, Detroit.

1969

- March 1: Mickey Mantle of the New York Yankees announces his retirement.
- April 14: Montreal Expos outfielder Mack Jones hit a three-run home run and two-run triple that highlighted an 8-7 win over the St. Louis Cardinals in the Expos' first home victory as a franchise at Jarry Park. Jones' blast was also the first MLB home run hit outside the United States.
- July 20: San Francisco Giants pitcher Gaylord Perry, six years after quipping, "They'll put a man on the moon before I hit a home run," hits the first and only home run of his career just hours after Neil Armstrong lands on the moon.
- World Series: the New York Mets win 4 games to 1 over the Baltimore Orioles.

BASEBALL

1970

- January 16: Gold Glove outfielder Curt Flood files a civil lawsuit challenging baseball's reserve clause, a suit that will have historic implications. Flood refused to report to the Phillies after he was traded by the Cardinals, contending the baseball rule violates federal antitrust laws.
- January 17: The Sporting News names Willie Mays as Player of the Decade for the 1960s.
- January 20: Lou Boudreau is elected to the Hall of Fame, receiving 232 of a possible 300 votes from the BBWAA.
- June 12: Dock Ellis of the Pittsburgh Pirates throws a no-hitter against the San Diego Padres. It is later revealed that he did so while under the influence of LSD.
- Robert W. Peterson's book *Only the Ball was White* is published. The book brings pressure on Major League Baseball to recognize the African-American players from Negro league baseball by honoring its stars in the Baseball Hall of Fame.
- World Series: The American League's Baltimore Orioles win their second World Title by defeating the National League's Cincinnati Reds, 4 games to 1.

1971

- World Series: Pittsburgh Pirates won 4 games to 3 over the Baltimore Orioles. Game four was the first night game in World Series history.

1972

- January 19: The BBWAA elects Sandy Koufax (344 votes), Yogi Berra (339), and Early Wynn (301) to the Hall of Fame. Koufax makes it in his first try and, at 36, is the youngest honoree in history. He won three Cy Young awards in a four-year span when the honor was only given to one pitcher for both leagues. Berra played in 14 World Series (ten world champions), he had more hits in Series play than any other player, and he was a three-time MVP for the Yankees. Wynn won 300 career games, and won 20 games five times. *September 30: Roberto Clemente got his 3,000th hit against the New York Mets.
- Sparky Lyle saves 35 games for the New York Yankees, breaking Ron Perranoski's 1970 records for AL pitchers and lefthanders. Lyle also becomes the first left-hander to save 100 career games in the American League.
- World Series: Oakland Athletics win their 6th World Championship by defeating the Cincinnati Reds, 4 games to 3.
- December 31 - The Pittsburgh Pirates' legendary right fielder Roberto Clemente dies in a plane crash near Puerto Rico on his way to bring relief supplies to Nicaraguan earthquake victims.

1973

- January 18: Orlando Cepeda signs with the Boston Red Sox, making him the first player signed by a team *specifically to be a* designated hitter.
- The American League uses the designated hitter rule for the first time. Ron Blomberg is the first player to bat as a DH.
- World Series: Oakland Athletics won 4 games to 3 over the New York Mets

BASEBALL

1974

- January 16: Former Yankees teammates Mickey Mantle and Whitey Ford are inducted into the Baseball Hall of Fame. Mantle becomes only the seventh player to make it in his first try. His 536 home runs with the Yankees ranked second only to Babe Ruth and he played in more games (2,401) than any other pinstriper, including Lou Gehrig. Ford was arguably the greatest Yankees pitcher of all time, retiring with more wins (236), more innings (3,171), more strikeouts (1,956), and more shutouts (45) than anyone in club history.
- Frank Robinson becomes the first African-American manager in Major League Baseball.
- April 8: Hank Aaron hit home run# 715 in the fourth inning off Los Angeles Dodgers pitcher Al Downing breaking Babe Ruth's career home run record.
- June 4 - The Cleveland Indians hosted "Ten Cent Beer Night", but had to forfeit the game to the Texas Rangers due to drunken and unruly fans.
- World Series: Oakland Athletics win 4 games to 1 over the Los Angeles Dodgers.

1975

- January 23: Slugger Ralph Kiner is inducted into the Baseball Hall of Fame.
- September 16: Pirates second baseman Rennie Stennett ties Wilbert Robinson's ML record, set June 10, 1892, by going 7-for-7 in a 9-inning game. He scored five of his club's runs in a 22-0 massacre of the Cubs, a major-league record for the biggest score in a shutout game in the 20th century.
- World Series: Cincinnati Reds win 4 games to 3 over the Boston Red Sox. Often described as one of the most memorable of all World Series.

1976

- April 25 - Chicago Cubs outfielder Rick Monday rescues an American flag just as two protestors are about to burn it in the outfield during a game at Dodger Stadium.
- Sparky Lyle breaks Hoyt Wilhelm's American League record of 154 career saves.
- World Series: The Cincinnati Reds (aka the "Big Red Machine") sweep the New York Yankees, 4 games to 0, to win their second straight championship.

1977

- January 19: Ernie Banks is elected to the Baseball Hall of Fame in his first year of eligibility. He won back-to-back MVP awards, but is best remembered for his famous line, "Let's play two".
- Sparky Lyle breaks Ron Perranoski's major league record for left-handers of 179 career saves.
- The Major League Baseball expansion Seattle Mariners and Toronto Blue Jays make their debuts (both are American League teams).
- World Series: The New York Yankees defeat the Los Angeles Dodgers. This is the Series in which Reggie Jackson becomes known as "Mr. October."

BASEBALL

1978

- World Series: New York Yankees win 4 games to 2 over the Los Angeles Dodgers. The Series MVP is Bucky Dent, New York

1979

- January 23: Willie Mays receives 409 of 432 votes in the BBWAA election to earn enshrinement in the Hall of Fame.
- World Series: Pittsburgh Pirates won 4 games to 3 over the Baltimore Orioles. The Series MVP was Willie Stargell, Pittsburgh

1980

- September 18: Outfielder Gary Ward become the sixth Minnesota Twins player to hit for the cycle. The Twins lose 9-8 to the Milwaukee Brewers, wasting Ward's effort. On May 26, 2004 his son, Daryle Ward, will repeat the feat guiding the Pirates' 11-8 victory over the Cardinals. Ward joined his father to become the first father-son combination in major league history to hit for the cycle.
- Rollie Fingers breaks Hoyt Wilhelm's major league record of 250 saves
- World Series: The Philadelphia Phillies of the National League end 97 years of frustration by defeating the American League champion Kansas City Royals.
- Japan's Sadaharu Oh retires from the Yomiuri Giants as the all time professional baseball home run king.

1981

- For a Venezuelans baseball player's strike the Caribbean World Series of this year is cancelled.
- January 15 - In his first year of eligibility, former Cardinals pitcher Bob Gibson is the only player elected to the Baseball Hall of Fame. Gibson won 20 games five times, struck out 3,117 batters, and captured the Cy Young Award and MVP in 1968 with a 1.12 ERA. Players falling short of the 301 votes needed for election include Don Drysdale (243), Gil Hodges (241), Harmon Killebrew (239), Hoyt Wilhelm (238), and Juan Marichal (233). All except Hodges would subsequently gain election.
- April 18 - An International League game between the Pawtucket Red Sox and the visiting Rochester Red Wings set the record for the most innings ever played in a single professional baseball game, at 33 innings (24 extra innings). The game was suspended after 32 innings on the morning of April 19, and was concluded on June 23 with a 3-2 Pawtucket victory.
- June 12 - Major League Baseball players begin a 49 day strike over the issue of free-agent compensation.
- World Series: Los Angeles Dodgers win 4 games to 2 over the New York Yankees. The Series MVP is a tie between Ron Cey, Pedro Guerrero and Steve Yeager, Los Angeles

BASEBALL

1982

- July 13: Montreal hosts the first MLB All-Star Game outside the United States. Reds SS Dave Concepción hits a 2-run home run in the 2nd inning to spark the National League to its 11th consecutive win over the American League 4-1. The NL has now won 19 of the last 20 contests. Concepción was named the MVP.
- August 18: Pete Rose sets record with his 13,941st plate appearance.
- World Series: St. Louis Cardinals won 4 games to 3 over the Milwaukee Brewers. The Series MVP was Cardinals catcher Darrell Porter.

1983

- January 12 - Brooks Robinson and Juan Marichal are elected to the Hall of Fame. Robinson, winner of 16 straight Gold Glove Awards and hero of the 1970 World Series, becomes the 14th player elected in his first year of eligibility. Marichal, the winningest Latin American pitcher in major league history, won 20 or more games six times and had an ERA of 2.50 or less six times.
- World Series: - Baltimore Orioles win their most recent World Series 4 games to 1 over the Philadelphia Phillies

1984

- January 10 - Luis Aparicio, Harmon Killebrew, and Don Drysdale are elected to the Baseball Hall of Fame
- World Series: - Detroit Tigers win 4 games to 1 over the San Diego Padres

1985

- Cincinnati Reds' player/manager Pete Rose breaks Ty Cobb's All-Time Hit Record of 4,191 hits. Rose's record-breaking single was off of San Diego Padres pitcher Eric Show (September 11)
- Rollie Fingers breaks Sparky Lyle's American League career record of 232 saves.
- World Series: The Kansas City Royals defeat the St. Louis Cardinals 4 games to 3, becoming the first team to win the World Series after losing the first two games at home.

1986

- All-Star Game: American League Manager Dick Howser is diagnosed with brain cancer after mixing up signals during the game.
- Dave Righetti saves 46 games for the New York Yankees, breaking a record shared by Dan Quisenberry and Bruce Sutter.
- October 27 - World Series: The New York Mets win 4 games to 3 over the Boston Red Sox.

BASEBALL

1987

- January 14: Catfish Hunter and Billy Williams are elected to the Baseball Hall of Fame. Hunter made his name as the ace of the Oakland A's staff in their championship years and made his fortune as one of the first free agents. Williams set an National League record by playing in 1,117 consecutive games and accumulating 426 home runs and a batting title.
- August 3: Minnesota Twins pitcher Joe Niekro is suspended for 10 days for possessing a nail file on the pitcher's mound. Niekro claimed he had been filing his nails in the dugout and put the file in his back pocket when the inning started.
- World Series: Minnesota Twins won 4 games to 3 over the St. Louis Cardinals. The Series MVP was Frank Viola, Minnesota
    - Lowest regular-season record of any World Series champion (85-77, .525)
    - First World Series game played indoors (Game 1 at the Hubert H. Humphrey Metrodome)
    - First World Series where the home team won every game

1988

- January 12: Former Pirates slugger Willie Stargell is the only player elected to the Baseball Hall of Fame. Stargell, leader of two world champions in Pittsburgh and NL co-MVP in 1979 at age 39, becomes the 17th player to be elected in his first year of eligibility. Jim Bunning falls four votes shy of the 321 needed for election in his 13th year on the ballot.
- August 9: The first night game ever at Wrigley Field is played. After an attempt the previous night was rained out, the Cubs defeat the New York Mets 6-4.
- World Series: Los Angeles Dodgers won 4 games to 1 over the Oakland Athletics. The Series MVP was Orel Hershiser, Los Angeles

1989

- April 8 - One-handed pitcher Jim Abbott makes his major-league debut with the California Angels, without spending a single day in the minor leagues. He went on to a 12-12 record for the season.
- August 10 - Ten months after undergoing surgery for cancer in his pitching arm, San Francisco Giants pitcher Dave Dravecky returns to the major leagues, winning his comeback 4-3.
- August 15 - Dave Dravecky's comeback bid ends tragically when his pitching arm breaks in the sixth inning of his second start. Two years later, the cancer-stricken arm would be amputated.
- August 24 - Following an investigation that he gambled on baseball, superstar player Pete Rose is banned from baseball for life.
- World Series: Oakland Athletics won 4 games to 0 over the San Francisco Giants. The Series MVP was Dave Stewart, Oakland.

1990

- Cincinnati Reds World Series (4-0) over Oakland Athletics. Cincinnati Reds NL Championship Series (4-2) over Pittsburgh Pirates

BASEBALL

1991

- Dave Righetti breaks Sparky Lyle's major league record for left-handers of 238 career saves.
- July 28 - Dennis Martinez of the Montreal Expos pitches the 13th perfect game in major league history, beating the Los Angeles Dodgers 2-0.
- World Series: The Minnesota Twins win 4 games to 3 over the Atlanta Braves. The series MVP is Jack Morris of Minnesota.

1992

- World Series - Toronto Blue Jays won 4 games to 2 over the Atlanta Braves. The Series MVP is Pat Borders, Toronto.
- The Toronto Blue Jays became the first Canadian team to play in a World Series and the first non-American team to win the World Series.

1993

- The Colorado Rockies and Florida Marlins play their inaugural season.
- Randy Myers saves 53 games for the Chicago Cubs, breaking Dave Righetti's record for left-handers.
- Lee Smith breaks the all-time save mark by recording his 358th save in a 9-7 win against the Los Angeles Dodgers on April 13.
- World Series: The Toronto Blue Jays win 4 games to 2 over the Philadelphia Phillies. The Series MVP is Paul Molitor, Toronto. Joe Carter hit the second ever walk-off home run to end the World Series.

1994

- A strike by baseball players results in the premature termination of the season and the cancellation of the Baseball World Series, for the first time since 1904.
- January 12: Steve Carlton, winner of 329 games and four Cy Young Awards, is elected to the Baseball Hall of Fame.
- June 22: OF Ken Griffey Jr. leads the Mariners to a 12-3 win over the Angels by stroking his 31st home run of the season. In doing so, Griffey Jr. breaks Babe Ruth's record for most home runs before the end of June.
- September 14: A labor strike by Major League Baseball players results in the premature termination of the season, and the cancellation of the World Series for the first time since 1904. The Montreal Expos were the league-leading team up to the strike, with a 74-40 record.
- Mets pitcher John Franco breaks Dave Righetti's major league record for left-handers of 252 career saves.
- The Richmond Braves win the International League championship.
- The Albuquerque Dukes win the Pacific Coast League championship.
- The Indianapolis Indians win the American Association championship.
- The Winnipeg Goldeyes win the Northern League championship.
- The Yomuiri Giants win the Japan Series, and in the view of the baseball media, are World Champions.

BASEBALL

1995

- World Series: Atlanta Braves won 4 games to 2 over the Cleveland Indians. The Series MVP was Tom Glavine, Atlanta
- September 6 - Cal Ripken Jr. breaks Lou Gehrig's record of playing 2131 consecutive games.

1996

- January 8 - For the first time in 25 years, no one garners 75 percent of the votes needed to be elected to the Baseball Hall of Fame. Phil Niekro comes closest with 68 percent.
- World Series: New York Yankees won 4 games to 2 over the Atlanta Braves. The Series MVP was relief pitcher, John Wetteland, New York

1997

- June 12 - Interleague play begins in baseball, ending a 126-year tradition of separating the major leagues until the World Series.
- World Series: Florida Marlins won 4 games to 3 over the Cleveland Indians. The Series MVP was Liván Hernández, Florida

1998

- Mark McGwire and Sammy Sosa each chase the home run record set previously by Roger Maris in 1961. Both men end up breaking the record; McGwire with 70 and Sosa with 66.
- World Series: New York Yankees win 4 games to 0 over the San Diego Padres. The Series MVP is Scott Brosius, New York

1999

- May 10: The Boston Red Sox pound the Seattle Mariners, 12-4, as shortstop Nomar Garciaparra leads the way with three home runs, including two grand slams. Garciaparra drives home 10 of Boston's runs as he clouts a bases loaded homer in the 1st, a 2-run shot in the 3rd, and another grand slam in the 8th. Nomar is the first Bosox since Jim Tabor, in 1939, to slam two slams in a game, and just the 9th in MLB history. Robin Ventura last did it, in 1995.
- World Series: New York Yankees won 4 games to 0 over the Atlanta Braves. The series MVP: Mariano Rivera, New York

2000

- World Series: New York Yankees win 4 games to 1 over the New York Mets. The Series MVP is Derek Jeter, of the Yankees

BASKETBALL

1950

- First FIBA World Championship. Argentina World Champion

1951

- NCAA Men's Basketball Championship:
    - Kentucky wins 68-58 over Kansas State University
- NBA Finals:
    - Rochester Royals won 4 games to 3 over the New York Knicks
- Amateur Basketball Association:
    - Basketball Jones single handedly beats the Harlem Globetrotters
- The seventh European basketball championship, Eurobasket 1951, is won by the Soviet Union.

1952

- NCAA Men's Basketball Championship:
    - Kansas wins 80-63 over St. John's
- NBA Finals|NBA Finals:
    - Minneapolis Lakers won 4 games to 3 over the Syracuse Nationals

1953

- NCAA Men's Basketball Championship:
    - Indiana wins 69-68 over Kansas
- NBA Finals|NBA Finals:
    - Minneapolis Lakers won 4 games to 1 over the New York Knicks
- The eighth European basketball championship, Eurobasket 1953, is won by the Soviet Union.
- The fifteenth South American Basketball Championship in Montevideo is won by Uruguay.

1954

- FIBA World Championship:
    - USA World Champion
- NCAA Men's Basketball Championship:
    - La Salle wins 92-76 over Bradley
- NBA Finals|NBA Finals:
    - Minneapolis Lakers win 4-3 over the Syracuse Nationals
- March 13: Milan High School, enrollment 161, defeated Muncie Central High School (enrollment over 1,600) 32-30 to win the Indiana state title. The 1986 movie classic *Hoosiers* was very loosely based on the story of this Milan team.

BASKETBALL

1955

- NCAA Men's Basketball Championship:
    - San Francisco wins 76-73 over La Salle
- NBA Finals|NBA Finals:
    - Syracuse Nationals win 4-3 over the Fort Wayne Pistons
- The ninth European basketball championship, Eurobasket 1955, is won by Hungary.
- March 1: Allen Fieldhouse opens at the University of Kansas as the Jayhawks defeat Kansas State

1956

- NCAA Men's Basketball Championship:
    - San Francisco wins 83-71 over Iowa
- NBA Finals|NBA Finals:
    - Philadelphia Warriors won 4 games to 1 over the Fort Wayne Pistons

1957

- NCAA Men's Division I Basketball Championship:
    - North Carolina wins 54-53 over Kansas
- NBA Finals:
    - Boston Celtics won 4 games to 3 over the St. Louis Hawks
- The tenth European basketball championship, Eurobasket 1957, is won by the Soviet Union.

1958

- NCAA Men's Basketball Championship:
    - Kentucky wins 84-72 over Seattle
- NBA Finals|NBA Finals:
    - St. Louis Hawks win 4 games to 2 over the Boston Celtics
- World Basketball Championships (Men) - Rio de Janeiro, Brazil
    - Gold: United States of America
    - Silver: Brazil
    - Bronze: Philippines

1959

- FIBA World Championship
    - Brazil World Champion
- NCAA Men's Basketball Championship:
    - California wins 71-70 over West Virginia
- NBA Finals|NBA Finals:
    - Boston Celtics win 4 games to 0 over the Minneapolis Lakers

BASKETBALL

1960

- NCAA Men's Basketball Championship:
    - Ohio St. wins 75-55 over California
- NBA Finals|NBA Finals:
    - Boston Celtics win 4 games to 3 over the St. Louis Hawks

1961

- NCAA Men's Basketball Championship:
    - Cincinnati wins 70-65 over Ohio St.
- NBA Finals NBA Finals:
    - Boston Celtics won 4 games to 1 over the St. Louis Hawks

1962

- March 2 - In Hershey, Pennsylvania, Wilt Chamberlain of the Philadelphia Warriors scored 100 points against the New York Knicks, breaking several National Basketball Association records.
- NCAA Men's Division I Basketball Championship:
    - Cincinnati wins 71-59 over Ohio St.
- NBA Finals:
    - Boston Celtics won 4 games to 3 over the Los Angeles Lakers

1963

- NCAA Men's Basketball Championship:
    - Loyola (Illinois) wins 60-58 over Cincinnati
- NBA Finals|NBA Finals:
    - Boston Celtics win 4 games to 2 over the Los Angeles Lakers
- FIBA World Championship:
    - Brazil World Champion

1964

- NCAA Men's Basketball Championship:
    - UCLA wins 97-83 over Duke
- NBA Finals|NBA Finals:
    - Boston Celtics won 4 games to 1 over the San Francisco Warriors

BASKETBALL

1965

- NCAA Men's Basketball Championship:
    - UCLA wins 91-80
- NBA Finals|NBA Finals:
    - Boston Celtics win 4 games to 1 over the Los Angeles Lakers

1966

- NCAA Men's Division I Basketball Championship:
    - Texas Western wins 72-65 over Kentucky
- NBA Finals|NBA Finals:
    - Boston Celtics won 4 games to 3 over the Los Angeles Lakers

1967

- NCAA Men's Division I Basketball Championship:
    - UCLA wins 79-64 over Dayton. This would be the first of an unprecedented seven consecutive titles for the Bruins.
- NBA Finals|NBA Finals:
    - Philadelphia 76ers won 4 games to 2 over the San Francisco Warriors
- FIBA World Championship
    - USSR World Champion

1968

- NCAA Men's Basketball Championship:
    - UCLA wins 78-55 over North Carolina
- NBA Finals|NBA Finals:
    - Boston Celtics won 4 games to 2 over the Los Angeles Lakers

1969

- NCAA Men's Basketball Championship:
    - UCLA wins 92-72 over Purdue
- NBA Finals|NBA Finals:
    - Boston Celtics won 4 games to 3 over the Los Angeles Lakers

BASKETBALL

1970

- NCAA Men's Division I Basketball Championship:
  - UCLA wins 80-69 over Jacksonville
- NBA Finals:
  - New York Knicks won 4 games to 3 over the Los Angeles Lakers
- FIBA World Championship
  - Yugoslavia World Champion

1971

- NCAA Men's Division I Basketball Championship:
  - UCLA wins 68-62 over Villanova
- NBA Finals:
  - Milwaukee Bucks win 4 games to 0 over the Baltimore Bullets

1972

- NCAA Men's Division I Basketball Championship:
  - UCLA wins 81-76 over Florida St.
- NBA Finals:
  - Los Angeles Lakers won 4 games to 1 over the New York Knicks

1973

- NCAA Men's Division I Basketball Championship:
  - UCLA wins 87-66 over Memphis State.
- NBA Finals:
  - New York Knicks won 4 games to 1 over the Los Angeles Lakers

1974

- NCAA Men's Division I Basketball Championship:
  - North Carolina State wins 76-64 over Marquette
    - In the semifinals of this tournament, NC State defeated UCLA 80-77 in overtime, ending UCLA's record streak of seven national titles. The last previous tournament not won by the Bruins was the 1966 tournament.
- NBA Finals:
  - Boston Celtics win 4 games to 3 over the Milwaukee Bucks
- FIBA World Championship
  - USSR World Champion
- January 19 – Notre Dame defeats UCLA 71-70, ending the Bruins' record 88-game winning streak.

BASKETBALL

1975

- April 9 - Asia's first professional basketball league, the Philippine Basketball Association played its first game at the Araneta Coliseum.
- Darryl Dawkins becomes the first NBA player drafted out of high school.
- NCAA Men's Division I Basketball Championship:
    - UCLA wins 92-85 over Kentucky in John Wooden's final game as Bruins coach.
- NBA Finals:
    - Golden State Warriors win 4 games to 0 over the Washington Bullets

1976

- NCAA Men's Division I Basketball Championship:
    - Indiana wins 86-68 over Michigan
- NBA Finals:
    - Boston Celtics win 4 games to 2 over the Phoenix Suns
- October 26-Outdoor Basketball Association debuts

1977

- NCAA Men's Division I Basketball Championship:
    - Marquette wins 67-59 over North Carolina
- NBA Finals:
    - Portland Trail Blazers won 4 games to 2 over the Philadelphia 76ers

1978

- Wilt Chamberlain is elected to the Basketball Hall of Fame, along with coaches Sam Barry, Eddie Hickey, John McLendon, Ray Meyer and Pete Newell, and referee Jim Enright
- NCAA Men's Division I Basketball Championship:
    - Kentucky wins 94-88 over Duke
- NBA Finals:
    - Washington Bullets won 4 games to 3 over the Seattle SuperSonics
- FIBA World Championship
    - Yugoslavia World Champion

1979

- NCAA Men's Division I Basketball Championship:
    - Michigan St. wins 75-64 over Indiana St.
- NBA Finals:
    - Seattle SuperSonics, coached by Lenny Wilkins, won 4 games to 1 over the Washington Bulletsfor the only finals win in Seattle Supersonics history.
- National Basketball League (Australia):
    - The Australian NBL was founded. The St Kilda Saints became the first champions by defeating the Canberra Cannons 94-93 in the final.

BASKETBALL

1980

- NCAA Men's Division I Basketball Championship:
    - Louisville wins 59-54 over UCLA
- NBA Finals:
    - Los Angeles Lakers won 4 games to 2 over the Philadelphia 76ers
- National Basketball League (Australia) Finals:
    - St. Kilda Saints defeated the West Adelaide Bearcats 113-88 in the final.

1981

- NCAA Men's Division I Basketball Championship:
    - Indiana wins 63-50 over North Carolina
- NBA Finals:
    - Boston Celtics won 4 games to 2 over the Houston Rockets
- National Basketball League (Australia) Finals:
    - Launceston Casino City defeated the Nunawading Spectres 75-54 in the final.

1982

- NCAA Men's Basketball Championship:
    - North Carolina wins 63-62 over Georgetown
- NBA Finals|NBA Finals:
    - Los Angeles Lakers won 4 games to 2 over the Philadelphia 76ers
- National Basketball League (Australia) Finals:
    - West Adelaide Bearcats defeated the Geelong Cats 80-74 in the final.
- FIBA World Championship
    - USSR World Champion

1983

- NCAA Men's Basketball Championship:
    - North Carolina State wins 54-52 over Houston
- NBA Finals|NBA Finals:
    - Philadelphia 76ers won 4 games to 0 over the Los Angeles Lakers
- National Basketball League (Australia) Finals:
    - Canberra Cannons defeated the West Adelaide Bearcats 75-73 in the final.

BASKETBALL

1984

- NCAA Men's Basketball Championship:
    - Georgetown wins 84-75 over Houston
- NBA Finals|NBA Finals:
    - Boston Celtics won 4 games to 3 over the Los Angeles Lakers
- National Basketball League (Australia) Finals:
    - Canberra Cannons defeated the Brisbane Bullets 84-82 in the final.
- Central Missouri State University won the NCAA Division II men's and women's basketball titles, becoming the first school ever in any division to accomplish the feat. The University of Connecticut would do the same in Division I in 2004.
- NBA Finals Draft]]:
    - A new era in the NBA is born on June 23 with the drafting of Houston's Hakeem Olajuwon, North Carolina's Michael Jordan and Auburn's Charles Barkley.

1985

- April |NCAA Men's Basketball Championship:
    - Villanova wins 66-64 over Georgetown
- NBA Finals Draft]]
    - Patrick Ewing was drafted, adding the final piece of the puzzle to the NBA, increasing its already immense popularity.
- NBA Finals|NBA Finals:
    - Los Angeles Lakers win 4 games to 2 over the Boston Celtics
- National Basketball League (Australia) Finals:
    - Brisbane Bullets defeated the Adelaide 36ers 121-95 in the final.
- the United States Basketball League (USBL) was founded

1986

- NCAA Men's Basketball Championship:
    - Louisville wins 72-69 over Duke
- NBA Finals Finals]]:
    - June - Boston Celtics win 4 games to 2 over the Houston Rockets
- National Basketball League (Australia) Finals:
    - Adelaide 36ers defeated the Brisbane Bullets 2-1 in the best-of-three final series.
- FIBA World Championship
    - USA World Champion

1987

- NCAA Men's Basketball Championship:
    - Indiana wins 74-73 over Syracuse
- NBA Finals|NBA Finals:
    - Los Angeles Lakers won 4 games to 2 over the Boston Celtics
- National Basketball League (Australia) Finals:
    - Brisbane Bullets defeated the Perth Wildcats 2-0 in the best-of-three final series.

BASKETBALL

1988

- NCAA Men's Basketball Championship:
  - Kansas wins 83-79 over Oklahoma
- NBA Finals|NBA Finals:
  - Los Angeles Lakers won 4 games to 3 over the Detroit Pistons
- National Basketball League (Australia) Finals:
  - Canberra Cannons defeated the North Melbourne Giants 2-1 in the best-of-three final series.

1989

- NCAA Men's Basketball Championship:
  - Michigan wins 80-79 over Seton Hall in overtime
- NBA Finals|NBA Finals:
  - Detroit Pistons win 4 games to 0 over the Los Angeles Lakers to win the franchise's first championship.
- National Basketball League (Australia) Finals:
  - North Melbourne Giants defeated the Canberra Cannons 2-1 in the best-of-three final series.

1990

- National Basketball League (Australia) Finals:
  - Perth Wildcats defeated the Brisbane Bullets 2-1 in the best-of-three final series.

1991

- NCAA Men's Basketball Championship: Duke wins 72-65 over Kansas
- June 12 - NBA Finals|NBA Finals: Chicago Bulls win 4 games to 1 over the Los Angeles Lakers to earn the franchise's first championship.
- November 7 - Basketball player Magic Johnson announces he tested positive for the virus that causes AIDS, thus ending his career in the NBA.
- National Basketball League (Australia) Finals: Perth Wildcats defeated the Eastside Melbourne Spectres 2-1 in the best-of-three final series.

1992

- NCAA Men's Basketball Championship: Duke wins 71-51 over Michigan
- NBA Finals|NBA Finals: Chicago Bulls win 4 games to 2 over the Portland Trail Blazers
- National Basketball League (Australia) Finals: South East Melbourne Magic defeated the Melbourne Tigers 2-1 in the best-of-three final series.

BASKETBALL

1993

- NCAA Men's Basketball Championship:
  - North Carolina wins 77-71 over Michigan
- NBA Finals NBA Finals:
  - Chicago Bulls win 4 games to 2 over the Phoenix Suns to complete their first three-peat of the decade (see John Paxson). Michael Jordan announced his retirement on October 6. He later went on to lead a great life at a strip bar.
- National Basketball League (Australia) Finals:
  - Melbourne Tigers defeated the Perth Wildcats 2-1 in the best-of-three final series.

1994

- NBA Finals NBA Finals:
  - The Knicks took a 3-2 lead on the Houston Rockets and had a chance to clinch it in Game 6 but John Starks' final shot was blocked by Hakeem Olajuwon. The Rockets would win game 7 and win their first NBA Championship. During Game 5 (June 17, 1994) most NBC affiliates (with the noted exception being the network's own flagship station.

1995

- NCAA Men's Basketball Championship:
  - UCLA wins 89-78 over Arkansas
- NBA Finals NBA Finals:
  - Houston Rockets win 4 games to 0 over the Orlando Magic
- National Basketball League (Australia) Finals:
  - Perth Wildcats defeated the North Melbourne Giants 2-1 in the best-of-three final series.

1996

- April 1 - NCAA Men's Basketball Championship:
  - Kentucky wins 76-67 over Syracuse
- NBA Finals NBA Finals:
  - Chicago Bulls win 4 games to 2 over the Seattle SuperSonics, after a record-breaking 72-10 regular season.
- National Basketball League (Australia) Finals:
  - South East Melbourne Magic defeated the Melbourne Tigers 2-1 in the best-of-three final series.

BASKETBALL

2000

- NBA Finals:
    - Los Angeles Lakers win their first NBA title in twelve years, defeating the Indiana Pacers 4 games to 2.
- NCAA Men's Basketball Championship:
    - Michigan State wins 89-76 over Florida
- WNBA Finals:
    - Houston Comets win 2 games to 0 over the New York Liberty to complete their four-peat.
- National Basketball League (Australia) Finals:
    - Perth Wildcats defeated the Victoria Titans 2-0 in the best-of-three final series.

BOXING

1950

- January in London, Joey Maxim won the light-heavyweight world title, stopping champion Freddie Mills in 10 rounds.
- September 27 - Ezzard Charles retains his World Heavyweight Championship with a 15 round unanimous decision over Joe Louis in New York City.

1951

- July 10 - Randy Turpin becomes the middleweight boxing champion after defeating Sugar Ray Robinson.
- July 18, Pittsburgh, Pennsylvania - Jersey Joe Walcott knocks out Ezzard Charles in round 7.

1952

- June 25 at Yankee Stadium, Joey Maxim defeats Sugar Ray Robinson by knockout to retain his world light heavyweight title. This is the only knockout Robinson would ever suffer.
- September 23 at Philadelphia, Pennsylvania, Rocky Marciano knocked out Jersey Joe Walcott in the 13th round to win the World Heavyweight Championship.

1953

- September 24 in New York City - Rocky Marciano retains his World Heavyweight title with a TKO over Roland La Starza in the 11th round.
- October in New York City - *Bobo Olson* scored a 15 round decision over Randy Turpin to win the World Middleweight Championship

1954

- September 17 in New York City, Rocky Marciano retained his World Heavyweight title with an 8th round knockout of Ezzard Charles

1955

- September 21 in New York City, Rocky Marciano knocks out the Light-heavyweight champion Archie Moore in the 9th round to retain his World Heavyweight Championship.

1956

- March 19 - At age 48, Dutch boxer Bep van Klaveren contests his last match in Rotterdam.
- April 27 - Rocky Marciano retires as the only undefeated Heavyweight Champion of the world with a perfect record (49-0).
- November 30, in Chicago, Illinois - Floyd Patterson knocks out Archie Moore in the 5th round to win the vacant World Heavyweight title.

BOXING

1957

- September 23 - Carmen Basilio won the World Middleweight Championship by a 15 round decision over Sugar Ray Robinson.

1958

- December 10 - Light-heavyweight champion Archie Moore is knocked down three times in the first round and once more in the fifth round by Yvon Durelle but Moore held on to come back to knock out Durelle in the 11th round.

1959

- June 26 — in New York City, Ingemar Johansson scored a 3rd round TKO over Floyd Patterson to win the World Heavyweight Championship

1960

- March 16 - Flash Elorde won the world junior lightweight title with a seventh-round knockout of Harold Gomes in Quezon City, Philippines.
- June - Floyd Patterson recovered the world heavyweight title from Ingemar Johansson, becoming the first-ever boxer to do so.
- September 5 - Cassius Clay wins the gold medal in boxing at the Rome Olympic Games.

1961

- June 3 in Los Angeles, California - Emile Griffith knocked out Gaspar Ortega in the 12th round to retain the Welterweight Championship

1962

- March 24, 1962 - Emile Griffith regained the World Welterweight Championship by knocking out Benny the "Kid" Paret in the 12th round. Paret died ten days later on April 3, 1962 as a result of severe head injuries sustained in the fight.
- September 25, 1962 - Sonny Liston knocks out Floyd Patterson, two minutes and six seconds into the first round, to become World Heavyweight Champion.

1963

- July 22 in Las Vegas, Nevada, Sonny Liston won the Heavyweight Championship of the world by knocking out Floyd Patterson in the 1st round.
- World Cycling Championship: Benoni Beheyt of Belgium

BOXING

1964

- February 25 in Charlotte - Cassius Clay defeated Sonny Liston by TKO in the 8th round to win the World Heavyweight Championship.
- December 14 in Philadelphia, Pennsylvania, Joey Giardello won a 15 round decision over Rubin "Hurricane" Carter to win the World Middleweight Title.

1965

- March 30 - Jose Torres won the Light Heavyweight Championship of the World, stopping Willie Pastrano in nine rounds, at New York's Madison Square Garden.

1966

- April 25 at New York City, World Welterweight Champion Emile Griffith won a 15 round unanimous decision over Dick Tiger to also become the World Middleweight Champion.

1967

- May 9 - Muhammad Ali was stripped of his World Heavyweight Champion titles and was banned from boxing by the various commissions for his refusal to be inducted into the United States Army.

1968

- May 24 - Bob Foster knocked out Dick Tiger in the fourth round to win the World Light Heavyweight Championship.

1969

- June 23 - Joe Frazier scored a 7th round TKO over Jerry Quarry.
- October 18 - Jose Napoles retained the World Welterweight Championship in a 15 round decision over Emile Griffith.

1970

- February 15 - Carlos Cruz, Featherweight Boxing Champion died in a plane crash
- February 16 - Joe Frazier starts a heavyweight world boxing champion winning streak with the knock out of Jimmy Ellis in five rounds.

1971

- March 8 - Joe Frazier defeats Muhammad Ali in the first of three epic bouts. Frazier defends the World Heavyweight Championship in a star-studded Madison Square Garden.

BOXING

1972

- June 26 - Roberto Duran stopped Ken Buchanan in the thirteenth round to win the WBA Lightweight Championship.

1973

- January 22 - George Foreman beats Joe Frazier by a knockout in two rounds to lift the world's Heavyweight championship from Frazier. It is HBO Boxing's first telecast.

1974

- February 9 in Paris – Carlos Monzon retains his world Middleweight title by a knockout in round seven over world Welterweight champion Jose Napoles.
- August 17 to 30 – **First World Amateur Boxing Championships** held in Havana, Cuba
  - Light Flyweight (– 48 kg): Jorge Hernández (Cuba)
  - Flyweight (– 51 kg): Douglas Rodríguez (Cuba)
  - Bantamweight (– 54 kg): Wilfredo Gómez (Puerto Rico)
  - Featherweight (– 57 kg): Howard Davis (United States)
  - Lightweight (– 60 kg): Vassily Solomin (Soviet Union)
  - Light Welterweight (– 63.5 kg): Ayub Kalule (Uganda)
  - Welterweight (– 67 kg): Emilio Correa (Cuba)
  - Light Middleweight (– 71 kg): Rolando Garbey (Cuba)
  - Middleweight (– 75 kg): Rufat Riskiyev (Soviet Union)
  - Light Heavyweight (– 81 kg): Mate Parlov (Yugoslavia)
  - Heavyweight (> 81 kg): Teófilo Stevenson (Cuba)
- October 30 in Kinshasa, Zaire – Muhammad Ali regained the World Heavyweight title by knocking out George Foreman in the eighth round of what was called *The Rumble in the Jungle*.

1975

- October 1 in Manila, Philippines Muhammad Ali defeated Joe Frazier to maintain the Heavyweight Championship of the world. Known as the *Thrilla In Manila*, many regard it as the greatest fight in boxing history.

1976

- October 8 in São Paulo, Brazil, former world featherweight champion Eder Jofre fought his last fight, outpointing Mexico's Octavio (Famoso) Gomez in ten rounds.

1977

- After 13 years and 82 contests, including 14 title defences, World Middleweight Champion Carlos Monzon retired undefeated.

BOXING

1978

- February 15 – Leon Spinks defeats Muhammad Ali by decision in 15 rounds to win the world's Heavyweight title.
- May 6 to 20 – **Second World Amateur Boxing Championships** held in Belgrade, Yugoslavia
    - *Light Flyweight (- 48 kg):* Stephen Muchoki (Kenya)
    - *Flyweight (- 51 kg):* Henryk Średnicki (Poland)
    - *Bantamweight (- 54 kg):* Adolfo Horta (Cuba)
    - *Featherweight (- 57 kg):* Ángel Herrera (Cuba)
    - *Lightweight (- 60 kg):* Andeh Davidson (Nigeria)
    - *Light Welterweight (- 63,5 kg):* Valery Lvov (Soviet Union)
    - *Welterweight (- 67 kg):* Valery Rachkov (Soviet Union)
    - *Light Middleweight (- 71 kg):* Viktor Savchenko (Soviet Union)
    - *Middleweight (- 75 kg):* José Gómez (Cuba)
    - *Light Heavyweight (- 81 kg):* Sixto Soria (Cuba)
    - *Heavyweight (> 81 kg):* Teófilo Stevenson (Cuba)
- September 15 – Muhammad Ali recovers the world's Heavyweight title, beating Leon Spinks by decision in their rematch. It is the first time a boxer wins the world Heavyweight title for a third time.

1979

- September 28 in Las Vegas, Nevada, Larry Holmes retains his World Heavyweight title with an 11th round TKO of Earnie Shavers.
- November 3 also in Las Vegas, dual world championship undercard: Vito Antuofermo retains his world Middleweight title with a 15 round draw (tie) against Marvin Hagler, and Sugar Ray Leonard wins his first word title, beating WBC world Welterweight champion Wilfredo Benítez by knockout in round 15.

1980

- March 14 - 22 members of the United States Olympic boxing team died in a plane crash near Warsaw, Poland
- June 20- Roberto Duran defeats Sugar Ray Leonard by a 15 round decision to win boxing's WBC world Welterweight title.
- August 2- Thomas Hearns defeats Jose Pipino Cuevas by a knockout in round 2 to win boxing's WBA world Welterweight title and Yasutsune Uehara knocks out Samuel Serrano in round six to win the WBA's world Jr. Lightweight title in Detroit
- In Cincinnati, Aaron Pryor defeats Antonio Kid Pambele Cervantes by a knockout in round four to win the WBA's world Jr. Welterweight title.
- October 2- Larry Holmes defeats Muhammad Ali by a knockout in round eleven to retain boxing's WBC world Heavyweight title, in what would be Ali's last world title bout.
- November 25- In *The No Más Fight*, in New Orleans, Louisiana, Sugar Ray Leonard recovers the WBC's world Welterweight championship with an eight round technical knockout of Roberto Duran.

BOXING

1981

- April 11: Larry Holmes defeats Trevor Berbick by a unanimous decision to retain the WBC heavyweight title.
- August 21: Salvador Sanchez defeats Wilfredo Gómez by knockout in round eight to retain boxing's WBC world Featherweight title.(see: Salvador Sanchez vs. Wilfredo Gómez)
- September 16: Sugar Ray Leonard defeats Thomas Hearns by knockout in round 14 to unify boxing's world Welterweight title.
- October 3: Mike Weaver defeats James (Quick) Tillis by a unanimous decisin to retain the WBA/World Boxing Association heavyweight title.

1982

- May 4 to 15 – **Third World Amateur Boxing Championships** held in Munich, West Germany
  - *Light Flyweight (– 48 kg):* Ismail Mustafov (Bulgaria)
  - *Flyweight (– 51 kg):* Yuri Alexandrov (Soviet Union)
  - *Bantamweight (– 54 kg):* Floyd Favors (United States)
  - *Featherweight (– 57 kg):* Adolfo Horta (Cuba)
  - *Lightweight (– 60 kg):* Ángel Herrera (Cuba)
  - *Light Welterweight (– 63.5 kg):* Carlos García (Cuba)
  - *Welterweight (– 67 kg):* Mark Breland (United States)
  - *Light Middleweight (– 71 kg):* Aleksandr Koshkyn (Soviet Union)
  - *Middleweight (– 75 kg):* Bernardo Comas (Cuba)
  - *Light Heavyweight (– 81 kg):* Pablo Romero (Cuba)
  - *Heavyweight (– 91 kg):* Alexander Yagubkin (Soviet Union)
  - *Super Heavyweight (> 91 kg):* Tyrell Biggs (United States)
- June 11 – Larry Holmes defeats Gerry Cooney for the WBC Heavyweight title. Cooney, a white challenger, was dubbed "The White Hope" in what builded up to be a very racially toned fight, see Larry Holmes vs. Gerry Cooney.
- November 12 – Aaron Pryor defeats Alexis Arguello in what would later be called the *fight of the decade*. Pryor retained the WBA's world Jr. Welterweight title with a 14th round knockout
- November 13 – Ray Mancini defeats Duk Koo Kim by knockout in 14 rounds in a tragic fight. Kim died five days later and the fight's outcome brought many new resolutions to boxing.
- December 3 – The Carnival of Champions

1983

- May 20 - For the first time ever, two world Heavyweight champions defend their titles the same night, at the same place: Larry Holmes retains the WBC title defeating future two time world champion Tim Witherspoon, and Michael Dokes retains his WBA title with a 15 round draw (tie) against former world champion Mike Weaver.
- June 16 - Roberto Duran wins his third world title, knocking out WBA world Jr. Middleweight champion Davey Moore in eight rounds.
- November 10 - Marvin Hagler retains his unified world Middleweight title with a 15 round unanimous decision over Roberto Duran. It was 1983's most anticipated bout.

BOXING

1984

- March 31 - Wilfredo Gómez defeats Juan Laporte by a decision in 12 rounds to conquer the WBC's world Featherweight crown.
- June 15 - In the most anticipated bout of the year, Thomas Hearns, WBC world Jr. Middleweight champion, knocks out WBA world champion Roberto Duran in two rounds. The WBA elects not to sanction the bout, declaring their version of the title vacant instead.

1985

- April 15 - *The War*. Marvin Hagler knocks out Thomas Hearns in three rounds to retain the world's Middleweight title.
- August 10 - Hector Camacho defeats Jose Luis Ramirez to lift the WBC's world Lightweight title.
- September 21 - Michael Spinks beats Larry Holmes by a decision in 15 rounds to become the first world Light Heavyweight champion to win a world Heavyweight title.

1986

- March 10 in Las Vegas, Nevada – Marvin Hagler retained the World Middleweight Championship with an 11th round knockout of John Mugabi.
- May 8 to 18 – **Fourth World Amateur Boxing Championships** held in Reno, United States
    - *Light Flyweight (– 48 kg):* Juan Torres Odelin (Cuba)
    - *Flyweight (– 51 kg):* Pedro Orlando Reyes (Cuba)
    - *Bantamweight (– 54 kg):* Moon Sung-Kil (South Korea)
    - *Featherweight (– 57 kg):* Kelcie Banks (United States)
    - *Lightweight (– 60 kg):* Adolfo Horta (Cuba)
    - *Light Welterweight (– 63,5 kg):* Vassili Shyshov (Soviet Union)
    - *Welterweight (– 67 kg):* Kenneth Gould (United States)
    - *Light Middleweight (– 71 kg):* Angel Espinosa (Cuba)
    - *Middleweight (– 75 kg):* Darrin Allen (United States)
    - *Light Heavyweight (– 81 kg):* Pablo Romero (Cuba)
    - *Heavyweight (– 91 kg):* Félix Savón (Cuba)
    - *Super Heavyweight (> 91 kg):* Teófilo Stevenson (Cuba)
- November 22 – Mike Tyson knocks-out Trevor Berbick in a round 2 fight, becoming the youngest world heavyweight-boxing champion (He 20 years, 4 months old).

1987

- March 7 in Las Vegas, Nevada, Mike Tyson adds the WBA heavyweight title to his WBC belt when he beats James Smith in a 12 round decision.
- April 6 - Sugar Ray Leonard beats Marvin Hagler for boxing's world Middleweight championship.

BOXING

1988

- June 6 - In Las Vegas, Nevada, Iran Barkley knocked out Thomas Hearns in the 3rd round to win the WBC Middleweight Title.
- June 27 In what was dubbed *Superfight '88* Mike Tyson knocks out Michael Spinks in Atlantic City, New Jersey and defends the Undisputed Heavyweight Championship of the World.
- November 7 - In Las Vegas, Nevada, boxer Sugar Ray Leonard knocks out Donnie LaLonde.

1989

- February 11 - In Grenoble, France, René Jacquot won a 12 round decision over Donald Curry to win the World Welterweight Championship
- May 29 to June 3 - **28th European Amateur Boxing Championships** held in Athens, Greece
    - *Light Flyweight (- 48 kg):* Ivailo Marinov (Bulgaria)
    - *Flyweight (- 51 kg):* Yuri Arbaczakov (Soviet Union)
    - *Bantamweight (- 54 kg):* Serafim Todorov (Bulgaria)
    - *Featherweight (- 57 kg):* Kirkor Kirkorov (Bulgaria)
    - *Lightweight (- 60 kg):* Konstantin Tszyu (Soviet Union)
    - *Light Welterweight (- 63.5 kg):* Igor Ruznikov (Soviet Union)
    - *Welterweight (- 67 kg):* Siegfried Mehnert (East Germany)
    - *Light Middleweight (- 71 kg):* Israel Akopkochyan (Soviet Union)
    - *Middleweight (- 75 kg):* Henry Maske (East Germany)
    - *Light Heavyweight (- 81 kg):* Sven Lange (East Germany)
    - *Heavyweight (- 91 kg):* Arnold Vanderlyde (Netherlands)
    - *Super Heavyweight (+ 91 kg):* Ulli Kaden (East Germany)

1990

- February 11 - James Buster Douglas defeated Mike Tyson by a knockout in round 10 to win the world's unified Heavyweight title, in what many consider boxing's biggest upset ever.
- March 31 - *Thunder Meets Lightning*: Julio César Chávez defeated Meldrick Taylor to unify boxing's world junior welterweight title.

BOXING

1991

- May 7 to 12 – **29th European Amateur Boxing Championships** held in Gothenburg, Sweden
- *Light Flyweight (– 48 kg):* Ivailo Marinov (Bulgaria) *Flyweight (– 51 kg):* István Kovács (Hungary) *Bantamweight (– 54 kg):* Serafim Todorov (Bulgaria) *Featherweight (– 57 kg):* Paul Griffin (Ireland) *Lightweight (– 60 kg):* Vasile Nistor (Romania) *Light Welterweight (– 63.5 kg):* Konstantin Tszyu (Soviet Union) *Welterweight (– 67 kg):* Roberto Welin (Sweden) *Light Middleweight (– 71 kg):* Israel Akopkochyan (Soviet Union) *Middleweight (– 75 kg):* Sven Ottke (Germany) *Light Heavyweight (– 81 kg):* Dariusz Michalczewski (Germany) *Heavyweight (– 91 kg):* Arnold Vanderlyde (Netherlands) *Super Heavyweight (+ 91 kg):* Yevgeni Belousov (Soviet Union)
- June 1 at Palm Springs, California – Terry Norris knocked out Donald Curry in the 8th Round to win the WBC Super Welterweight Championship.
- August 2 to 18 – **Pan American Games** held in Havana, Cuba.
  - *Light Flyweight (– 48 kg):* Rogelio Marcelo (Cuba) *Flyweight (– 51 kg):* José Ramos (Cuba) *Bantamweight (– 54 kg):* Enrique Carrion (Cuba) *Featherweight (– 57 kg):* Arnaldo Mesa (Cuba) *Lightweight (– 60 kg):* Julio Gonzáles (Cuba) *Light Welterweight (– 63.5 kg):* Steve Johnston (United States) *Welterweight (– 67 kg):* Juan Hernández Sierra (Cuba) *Light Middleweight (– 71 kg):* Juan Carlos Lemus (Cuba) *Middleweight (– 75 kg):* Ramón Garbey (Cuba) *Light Heavyweight (– 81 kg):* Orestes Solano (Cuba) *Heavyweight (– 91 kg):* Félix Savón (Cuba) *Super Heavyweight (+ 91 kg):* Roberto Balado (Cuba)

1992

- November 13 – Riddick Bowe won a 12 round decision over Evander Holyfield to win the undisputed heavyweight championship.

1993

- March 13 – Michael Carbajal comes off the floor twice to knock out Humberto Gonzalez in seven rounds and unify the world's Jr. Flyweight title in *the fight of the year*
- May 7 to 16 – **World Amateur Boxing Championships** held in Tampere, Finland
  - *Light Flyweight (– 48 kg):* Nszan Munczyan (Armenia) *Flyweight (– 51 kg):* Waldemar Font (Cuba) *Bantamweight (– 54 kg):* Aleksandar Hristov (Bulgaria) *Featherweight (– 57 kg):* Serafim Todorov (Bulgaria) *Lightweight (– 60 kg):* Damian Austin (Cuba) *Light Welterweight (– 63.5 kg):* Héctor Vinent (Cuba) *Welterweight (– 67 kg):* Juan Hernández Sierra (Cuba) *Light Middleweight (– 71 kg):* Francisc Vaştag (Romania) *Middleweight (– 75 kg):* Ariel Hernández (Cuba) *Light Heavyweight (– 81 kg):* Ramón Garbey (Cuba) *Heavyweight (– 91 kg):* Félix Savón (Cuba) *Super Heavyweight (+ 91 kg):* Roberto Balado (Cuba)
- September 6 to 12 – **30th European Amateur Boxing Championships** held in Bursa, Turkey.
  - *Light Flyweight (– 48 kg):* Daniel Petrov (Bulgaria) *Flyweight (– 51 kg):* Ravchan Gusseynov (Azerbaijan) *Bantamweight (– 54 kg):* Raimkul Malakhbekov (Russia) *Featherweight (– 57 kg):* Serafim Todorov (Bulgaria) *Lightweight (– 60 kg):* Jacek Bielski (Poland) *Light Welterweight (– 63.5 kg):* Nurhan Süleymanoğlu (Turkey) *Welterweight (– 67 kg):* Vitalius Karpaciauskas (Lithuania) *Light Middleweight (– 71 kg):* Francisc Vaştag (Romania) *Middleweight (– 75 kg):* Dirk Eigenbrodt (Germany) *Light Heavyweight (– 81 kg):* Igor Schinin (Russia) *Heavyweight (– 91 kg):* Georgi Kandelaki (Georgia) *Super Heavyweight (+ 91 kg):* Svilen Rusinov (Bulgaria)
- November 12 – Evander Holyfield beats Riddick Bowe by decision in twelve rounds to regain the world's unified Heavyweight title. It is the *fan man fight*.

BOXING

1994

- January 29 - Frankie Randall causes Julio César Chávez his first defeat in 91 professional bouts, winning the WBC world Jr. Welterweight title in the process, by a split decision in 12 rounds.
- November 5 - Forty-five year old George Foreman becomes boxing's oldest heavyweight champion when he knocked out Michael Moorer in the 10th round of a Las Vegas, Nevada fight

1995

- March 11 to 27 – **Pan American Games** held in Mar del Plata, Argentina.
    - *Light Flyweight (– 48 kg):* Edgar Velásquez (Venezuela) *Flyweight (– 51 kg):* Juan Guzmán (Cuba) *Bantamweight (– 54 kg):* Juan Despaigne (Cuba) *Featherweight (– 57 kg):* Arnaldo Mesa (Cuba) *Lightweight (– 60 kg):* Julio Gonzáles (Cuba) *Light Welterweight (– 63.5 kg):* Walter Crucce (Argentina) *Welterweight (– 67 kg):* David Reid (United States) *Light Middleweight (– 71 kg):* Alfredo Duvergel (Cuba) *Middleweight (– 75 kg):* Ariel Hernández (Cuba) *Light Heavyweight (– 81 kg):* Antonio Tarver (United States) *Heavyweight (– 91 kg):* Félix Savón (Cuba) *Super Heavyweight (+ 91 kg):* Leonardo Martinez Fiz (Cuba)
- May 4 to 15 – **World Amateur Boxing Championships** held in Berlin, Germany
    - *Light Flyweight (– 48 kg):* Daniel Petrov (Bulgaria) *Flyweight (– 51 kg):* Zoltan Lunka (Germany) *Bantamweight (– 54 kg):* Raimkul Malakhbekov (Russia) *Featherweight (– 57 kg):* Serafim Todorov (Bulgaria) *Lightweight (– 60 kg):* Leonard Doroftei (Romania) *Light Welterweight (– 63.5 kg):* Héctor Vinent (Cuba) *Welterweight (– 67 kg):* Juan Hernández Sierra (Cuba) *Light Middleweight (– 71 kg):* Francisc Vastag (Romania) *Middleweight (– 75 kg):* Ariel Hernández (Cuba) *Light Heavyweight (– 81 kg):* Antonio Tarver (United States) *Heavyweight (– 91 kg):* Félix Savón (Cuba) *Super Heavyweight (+ 91 kg):* Alexei Lezin (Russia)
- May 6 – Oscar de la Hoya scored a second round TKO in Las Vegas, Nevada over Rafael Ruelas to retain his Lightweight Championship.

1996

- March 16 - Christy Martin defeats Deirdre Gogarty by a decision in six rounds to retain her Women's boxing world title in front of a national tv audience. This fight is credited with making the general public aware of women's boxing.
- March 30 to 7 – **31st European Amateur Boxing Championships** held in Vejle, Denmark.
    - *Light Flyweight (– 48 kg):* Daniel Petrov (Bulgaria) *Flyweight (– 51 kg):* Albert Pakeyev (Russia) *Bantamweight (– 54 kg):* István Kovács (Hungary) *Featherweight (– 57 kg):* Ramaz Paliani (Russia) *Lightweight (– 60 kg):* Leonard Doroftei (Romania) *Light Welterweight (– 63.5 kg):* Oktay Urkal (Germany) *Welterweight (– 67 kg):* Al Hassan (Denmark) *Light Middleweight (– 71 kg):* Francisc Vastag (Romania) *Middleweight (– 75 kg):* Sven Ottke (Germany) *Light Heavyweight (– 81 kg):* Pietro Aurino (Italy) *Heavyweight (– 91 kg):* Luan Krasniqi (Germany) *Super Heavyweight (+ 91 kg):* Alexei Lezin (Russia)
- June 7 - Oscar de la Hoya defeats Julio César Chávez by a knockout in four rounds to win the WBC's world Jr. Welterweight championship.

BOXING

1997

- January 18 – Oscar de la Hoya maintained his World Boxing Council super lightweight title in with a 12-round unanimous decision over Miguel Angel Gonzalez in Las Vegas, Nevada.
- June 28 – Mike Tyson bites off a piece of the ear of Evander Holyfield in the third round of their WBA Heavyweight title fight, getting disqualified by referee Mills Lane.
- July 9 – Mike Tyson's boxing license is suspended for at least a year and he is fined $3 million for biting Evander Holyfield's ear in a televised match.
- October 18 to 26 – **World Amateur Boxing Championships** held in Budapest, Hungary
  - *Light Flyweight (– 48 kg):* Maikro Romero (Cuba) *Flyweight (– 51 kg):* Manuel Mantilla (Cuba) *Bantamweight (– 54 kg):* Raimkul Malakhbekov (Russia) *Featherweight (– 57 kg):* István Kovács (Hungary) *Lightweight (– 60 kg):* Aleksander Maletin (Russia) *Light Welterweight (– 63.5 kg):* Dorel Simion (Romania) *Welterweight (– 67 kg):* Oleg Saitov (Russia) *Light Middleweight (– 71 kg):* Alfredo Duvergel (Cuba) *Middleweight (– 75 kg):* Zsolt Erdei (Hungary) *Light Heavyweight (– 81 kg):* Aleksandr Lebziak (Russia) *Heavyweight (– 91 kg):* Félix Savón (Cuba) *Super Heavyweight (+ 91 kg):* Georgi Kandalaki (Georgia)

1998

- May 17 to 24 – **32nd European Amateur Boxing Championships** held in Minsk, Belarus
  - *Light Flyweight (– 48 kg):* Sergey Kazakov (Russia) *Flyweight (– 51 kg):* Vladimir Sidorenko (Ukraine) *Bantamweight (– 54 kg):* Sergey Danilchenko (Ukraine) *Featherweight (– 57 kg):* Ramaz Paliani (Georgia) *Lightweight (– 60 kg):* Kay Huste (Germany) *Light Welterweight (– 63.5 kg):* Dorel Simion (Romania) *Welterweight (– 67 kg):* Oleg Saitov (Russia) *Light Middleweight (– 71 kg):* Frédéric Esther (France) *Middleweight (– 75 kg):* Zsolt Erdei (Hungary) *Light Heavyweight (– 81 kg):* Aleksandr Lebziak (Russia) *Heavyweight (– 91 kg):* Giacobbe Fragomeni (Italy) *Super Heavyweight (+ 91 kg):* Alexei Lezin (Russia)
- June 27 – Shane Mosley stopped Wilfrido Ruiz in the 5th round to retain the IBF Lightweight Championship.

BOXING

1999

- July 31 to August 8 – **Pan American Games** held in Winnipeg, Canada.
  - Light Flyweight (– 48 kg): Maikro Romero (Cuba) Flyweight (– 51 kg): Omar Andrés Narváez (Argentina) Bantamweight (– 54 kg): Gerald Tucker (United States) Featherweight (– 57 kg): Yudel Jhonson (Cuba) Lightweight (– 60 kg): Mario Kindelán (Cuba) Light Welterweight (– 63.5 kg): Victor Hugo Castro (Argentina) Welterweight (– 67 kg): Juan Hernández Sierra (Cuba) Light Middleweight (– 71 kg): Jorge Gutierrez (Cuba) Middleweight (– 75 kg): Yohanson Martinez (Cuba) Light Heavyweight (– 81 kg): Humberto Savigne (Cuba) Heavyweight (– 91 kg): Odlanier Solis (Cuba) Super Heavyweight (+ 91 kg): Alexis Rubalcaba (Cuba)
- August 20 to 27 – **World Amateur Boxing Championships** held in Houston, Texas in the United States
  - Light Flyweight (– 48 kg): Brian Viloria (United States) Flyweight (– 51 kg): Bulat Jumadilov (Kazakhstan) Bantamweight (– 54 kg): Crinu Olteanu (Romania) Featherweight (– 57 kg): Ricardo Juarez (United States) Lightweight (– 60 kg): Mario Kindelán (Cuba) Light Welterweight (– 63.5 kg): Mahammatkodir Abdoollayev (Uzbekistan) Welterweight (– 67 kg): Juan Hernández Sierra (Cuba) Light Middleweight (– 71 kg): Marian Simion (Romania) Middleweight (– 75 kg): Utkirbek Haydarov (Uzbekistan) Light Heavyweight (– 81 kg): Michael Simms (United States) Heavyweight (– 91 kg): Michael Bennett (United States) Super Heavyweight (+ 91 kg): Sinan Samil Sam (Turkey)
- September 18 – *The Fight of the Millennium*:
  - Félix Trinidad defeats Oscar de la Hoya by split 12 round decision to unify the IBF and WBC's world Welterweight championships.

2000

- May 13 to 21 – **33rd European Amateur Boxing Championships** held in Tampere, Finland
  - Light Flyweight (– 48 kg): Valeri Sidorenko (Ukraine) Flyweight (– 51 kg): Vladimir Sidorenko (Ukraine) Bantamweight (– 54 kg): Agasi Agagüloglu (Turkey) Featherweight (– 57 kg): Ramaz Paliani (Turkey) Lightweight (– 60 kg): Alexander Maletin (Bulgaria) Light Welterweight (– 63.5 kg): Alexei Leonov (Russia) Welterweight (– 67 kg): Bülent Ülüsoy (Turkey) Light Middleweight (– 71 kg): Adnan Ćatić (Germany) Middleweight (– 75 kg): Zsolt Erdei (Hungary) Light Heavyweight (– 81 kg): Aleksandr Lebziak (Russia) Heavyweight (– 91 kg): Jackson Chanet (France) Super Heavyweight (+ 91 kg): Alexei Lezin (Russia)
- July 29 – Kostya Tszyu defeats Julio César Chávez by a knockout in six to retain the WBC's world Jr. Welterweight title.
- August 12 – Evander Holyfield defeats John Ruiz by decision in 12 rounds to regain the WBA's world Heavyweight title, becoming the first boxer to win the world Heavyweight title four times.

FIGURE SKATING

1950

- World Figure Skating Championships:
    - Men's champion: Dick Button, United States
    - Ladies' champion: Aja Zanova, Czechoslovakia
    - Pair skating champions: Karol Kennedy & Michael Kennedy, United States

1951

- World Figure Skating Championships:
    - Men's champion: Dick Button, United States
    - Ladies' champion: Jeanette Altwegg, Great Britain
    - Pair skating champions: Ria Baran & Paul Falk, Germany

1952

- World Figure Skating Championships:
    - Men's champion: Dick Button, United States
    - Ladies' champion: Jacqueline du Bief, France
    - Pair skating champions: Ria Falk & Paul Falk, Germany
    - Ice dancing champions: Jean Westwood & Lawrence Demmy, Great Britain

1953

- World Figure Skating Championships:
    - Men's champion: Hayes Alan Jenkins, United States
    - Ladies' champion: Tenley Albright, United States
    - Pair skating champions: Jennifer Nicks & John Nicks, Great Britain
    - Ice dancing champions: Jean Westwood & Lawrence Demmy, Great Britain

1954

- World Figure Skating Championships:
    - Men's champion: Hayes Alan Jenkins, United States
    - Ladies' champion: Gundi Busch, Germany
    - Pair skating champions: Frances Dafoe & Norris Bowden, Canada
    - Ice dancing champions: Jean Westwood & Lawrence Demmy, Great Britain

1955

- World Figure Skating Championships:
    - Men's champion: Hayes Alan Jenkins, United States
    - Ladies' champion: Tenley Albright, United States
    - Pair skating champions: Frances Dafoe & Norris Bowden, Canada
    - Ice dancing champions: Jean Westwood & Lawrence Demmy, Great Britain

FIGURE SKATING

1956

- 1956 Winter Olympics:
    - Men's champion: Hayes Alan Jenkins, United States
    - Ladies' champion: Tenley Albright, United States
    - Pair skating champions: Elisabeth Schwartz & Kurt Oppelt, Austria
- World Figure Skating Championships:
    - Men's champion: Hayes Alan Jenkins, United States
    - Ladies' champion: Carol Heiss, United States
    - Pair skating champions: Elisabeth Schwartz & Kurt Oppelt, Austria
    - Ice dancing champions: Pamela Wright & Paul Thomas (skater), Great Britain
- European Figure Skating Championships:
    - Men's champion: Alain Giletti, France
    - Ladies' champion: Ingrid Wendl, Austria
    - Pair skating champions: Elisabeth Schwartz & Kurt Oppelt, Austria
    - Ice dancing champions: Pamela Wright & Paul Thomas (skater), Great Britain

1957

- World Figure Skating Championships:
    - Men's champion: David Jenkins, United States
    - Ladies' champion: Carol Heiss, United States
    - Pair skating champions: Barbara Wagner & Robert Paul, Canada
    - Ice dancing champions: June Markham & Courtney Jones, Great Britain

1958

- World Figure Skating Championships:
    - Men's champion: David Jenkins, United States
    - Ladies' champion: Carol Heiss, United States
    - Pair skating champions: Barbara Wagner & Robert Paul, Canada
    - Ice dancing champions: June Markham & Courtney Jones, Great Britain

1959

- World Figure Skating Championships:
    - Men's champion: David Jenkins, United States
    - Ladies' champion: Carol Heiss, United States
    - Pair skating champion: Barbara Wagner & Robert Paul, Canada
    - Ice dancing champion: Doreen Denny & Courtney Jones, Great Britain

FIGURE SKATING

1960

- World Figure Skating Championships:
    - Men's champion: Alain Giletti, France
    - Ladies' champion: Carol Heiss, United States
    - Pair skating champions: Barbara Wagner & Robert Paul, Canada
    - Ice dancing champions: Doreen Denny & Courtney Jones, Great Britain

1961

- The World Figure Skating Championships in Prague, Czechoslovakia were canceled after the entire United States team of skaters, officials, leaders and chaperones all died on February 15 in a plane crash just outside of Belgium while traveling to the competition.

1962

- World Figure Skating Championships
    - Men's champion: Donald Jackson, Canada
    - Ladies' champion: Sjoukje Dijkstra, Netherlands
    - Pair skating champions: Maria Jelinek & Otto Jelinek, Canada
    - Ice dancing champions: Eva Romanová & Pavel Roman, Czechoslovakia

1963

- World Figure Skating Championships
    - Men's champion: Donald McPherson, Canada
    - Ladies' champion: Sjoukje Dijkstra, Netherlands
    - Pair skating champions: Marika Kilius & Hans-Jürgen Bäumler, Germany
    - Ice dancing champions: Eva Romanová & Pavel Roman, Czechoslovakia

1964

- World Figure Skating Championships
    - Men's champion: Manfred Schnelldorfer, Germany
    - Ladies' champion: Sjoukje Dijkstra, Netherlands
    - Pair skating champions: Marika Kilius & Hans-Jürgen Bäumler, Germany
    - Ice dancing champions: Eva Romanová & Pavel Roman, Czechoslovakia

1965

- World Figure Skating Championships
    - Men's champion: Alain Calmat, France
    - Ladies' champion: Petra Burka, Canada
    - Pair skating champions: Ludmila Belousova & Oleg Protopopov, Soviet Union
    - Ice dancing champions: Eva Romanová & Pavel Roman, Czechoslovakia

FIGURE SKATING

1966

- World Figure Skating Championships:
    - Men's champion: Emmerich Dänzer, Austria
    - Ladies' champion: Peggy Fleming, United States
    - Pair skating champions: Ludmila Belousova & Oleg Protopopov, Soviet Union
    - Ice dancing champions: Diane Towler & Bernard Ford, Great Britain

1967

- World Figure Skating Championships:
    - Men's champion: Emmerich Dänzer, Austria
    - Ladies' champion: Peggy Fleming, United States
    - Pair skating champions: Ludmila Belousova & Oleg Protopopov, Soviet Union
    - Ice dancing champions: Diane Towler & Bernard Ford, Great Britain

1968

- World Figure Skating Championships:
    - Men's champion: Emmerich Dänzer, Austria
    - Ladies' champion: Peggy Fleming, United States
    - Pair skating champions: Ludmila Belousova & Oleg Protopopov, Soviet Union
    - Ice dancing champions: Diane Towler & Bernard Ford, Great Britain

1969

- World Figure Skating Championships:
    - Men's champion: Tim Wood, United States
    - Ladies' champion: Gabrielle Seyfert, Germany
    - Pair skating champions: Irina Rodnina & Alexei Ulanov, Soviet Union
    - Ice dancing champions: Diane Towler & Bernard Ford, Great Britain

1970

- World Figure Skating Championships:
    - Men's champion: Tim Wood, United States
    - Ladies' champion: Gabrielle Seyfert, Germany
    - Pair skating champions: Irina Rodnina & Alexei Ulanov, Soviet Union
    - Ice dancing champions: Lyudmila Pakhomova & Alexandr Gorshkov, Soviet Union

FIGURE SKATING

1971

- World Figure Skating Championships:
    - Men's champion: Ondrej Nepela, Czechoslovakia
    - Ladies' champion: Beatrix Schuba, Austria
    - Pair skating champions: Irina Rodnina & Alexei Ulyanov, Soviet Union
    - Ice dancing champions: Lyudmila Pakhomova & Alexandr Gorshkov, Soviet Union

1972

- World Figure Skating Championships:
    - Men's champion: Ondrej Nepela, Czechoslovakia
    - Ladies' champion: Beatrix Schuba, Austria
    - Pair skating champions: Irina Rodnina & Alexei Ulyanov, Soviet Union
    - Ice dancing champions: Lyudmila Pakhomova & Alexandr Gorshkov, Soviet Union

1973

- World Figure Skating Championships:
    - Men's champion: Ondrej Nepela, Czechoslovakia
    - Ladies' champion: Karen Magnussen, Canada
    - Pair skating champions: Irina Rodnina & Alexander Zaitsev, Soviet Union
    - Ice dancing champions: Lyudmila Pakhomova & Alexandr Gorshkov, Soviet Union

1974

- World Figure Skating Championships:
    - Men's champion: Jan Hoffmann, Germany
    - Ladies' champion: Christine Errath, Germany
    - Pair skating champions: Irina Rodnina & Alexander Zaitsev, Soviet Union
    - Ice dancing champions: Lyudmila Pakhomova & Alexandr Gorshkov, Soviet Union

1975

- World Figure Skating Championships:
    - Men's champion: Sergey Nikolayevich Volkov, Soviet Union
    - Ladies' champion: Dianne de Leeuw, Netherlands
    - Pair skating champions: Irina Rodnina & Alexander Zaitsev, Soviet Union
    - Ice dancing champions: Irina Moiseyeva & Andrei Minenkov, Soviet Union

FIGURE SKATING

1976

- World Figure Skating Championships:
  - Men's champion: John Curry, Britain
  - Ladies' champion: Dorothy Hamill, United States
  - Pair skating champions: Irina Rodnina & Alexander Zaitsev, Soviet Union
  - Ice dancing champions: Lyudmila Pakhomova & Alexandr Gorshkov, Soviet Union

1977

- World Figure Skating Championships:
  - Men's champion: Vladimir Kovalev, Soviet Union
  - Ladies' champion: Linda Fratianne, United States
  - Pair skating champions: Irina Rodnina & Alexander Zaitsev, Soviet Union
  - Ice dancing champions: Irina Moiseyeva & Andrei Minenkov, Soviet Union

1978

- World Figure Skating Championships:
  - Men's champion: Charles Tickner, United States
  - Ladies' champion: Anett Pötzsch, Germany
  - Pair skating champions: Irina Rodnina & Alexander Zaitsev, Soviet Union
  - Ice dancing champions: Natalia Linichuk & Gennadi Karponossov, Soviet Union

1979

- World Figure Skating Championships:
  - Men's champion: Vladimir Kovalev, Soviet Union
  - Ladies' champion: Linda Fratianne, United States
  - Pair skating champions: Tai Babilonia & Randy Gardner, United States
  - Ice dancing champions: Natalia Linichuk & Gennadi Karponossov, Soviet Union

1980

- World Figure Skating Championships:
  - Men's champion: Jan Hoffmann, Germany
  - Ladies' champion: Anett Pötzsch, Germany
  - Pair skating champions: Marina Cherkasova & Sergei Shakhrai, Soviet Union
  - Ice dancing champions: Krisztina Regöczy & Andras Sallay, Hungary

FIGURE SKATING

1981

- World Figure Skating Championships:
    - Men's champion: Scott Hamilton, United States
    - Ladies' champion: Denise Biellmann, Switzerland
    - Pair skating champions: Irina Vorobeva & Igor Lisovski, Soviet Union
    - Ice dancing champions: Jayne Torvill & Christopher Dean, Great Britain

1982

- World Figure Skating Championships:
    - Men's champion: Scott Hamilton, United States
    - Ladies' champion: Elaine Zayak, United States
    - Pair skating champions: Sabine Baeß & Tassilo Thierbach, Germany
    - Ice dancing champions: Jayne Torvill & Christopher Dean, Great Britain

1983

- World Figure Skating Championships:
    - Men's champion: Scott Hamilton, United States
    - Ladies' champion: Rosalynn Sumners, United States
    - Pair skating champions: Elena Valova & Oleg Vasiliev, Soviet Union
    - Ice dancing champions: Jayne Torvill & Christopher Dean, Great Britain

1984

- World Figure Skating Championships:
    - Men's champion: Scott Hamilton, United States
    - Ladies' champion: Katarina Witt, East Germany
    - Pair skating champions: Barbara Underhill & Paul Martini, Canada
    - Ice dancing champions: Jayne Torvill & Christopher Dean, Great Britain

1985

- World Figure Skating Championships:
    - Men's champion: Alexander Fadeev, Soviet Union
    - Ladies' champion: Katarina Witt, East Germany
    - Pair skating champions: Elena Valova / Oleg Vasiliev, Soviet Union
    - Ice dancing champions: Natalia Bestemianova / Andrei Bukin, Soviet Union

FIGURE SKATING

1986

- World Figure Skating Championships:
    - Men's champion: Brian Boitano, United States
    - Ladies' champion: Debi Thomas, United States
    - Pair skating champions: Ekaterina Gordeeva / Sergei Grinkov, Soviet Union
    - Ice dancing champions: Natalia Bestemianova / Andrei Bukin, Soviet Union

1987

- World Figure Skating Championships:
    - Men's champion: Brian Orser, Canada
    - Ladies' champion: Katarina Witt, Germany
    - Pair skating champions: Ekaterina Gordeeva / Sergei Grinkov, Soviet Union
    - Ice dancing champions: Natalia Bestemianova / Andrei Bukin, Soviet Union

1988

- World Figure Skating Championships:
    - Men's champion: Brian Boitano, United States
    - Ladies' champion: Katarina Witt, East Germany
    - Pair skating champions: Elena Valova / Oleg Vasiliev, Soviet Union
    - Ice dancing champions: Natalia Bestemianova / Andrei Bukin, Soviet Union

1989

- World Figure Skating Championships:
    - Men's champion: Kurt Browning, Canada
    - Ladies' champion: Midori Ito, Japan
    - Pair skating champions: Ekaterina Gordeeva & Sergei Grinkov, Soviet Union
    - Ice dancing champions: Marina Klimova / Sergei Ponomarenko, Soviet Union

1990

- World Figure Skating Championships:
    - Men's champion: Kurt Browning, Canada
    - Ladies' champion: Jill Trenary, United States
    - Pair skating champions: Ekaterina Gordeeva & Sergei Grinkov, Soviet Union
    - Ice dancing champions: Marina Klimova / Sergei Ponomarenko, Soviet Union

FIGURE SKATING

1991

- World Figure Skating Championships:
    - Men's champion: Kurt Browning, Canada
    - Ladies' champion: Kristi Yamaguchi, United States
    - Pair skating champions: Natalia Mishkutenok & Artur Dmitriev, Soviet Union
    - Ice dancing champions: Isabelle Duchesnay & Paul Duchesnay, France

1992

- World Figure Skating Championships:
    - Men's champion: Viktor Petrenko, Ukraine
    - Ladies' champion: Kristi Yamaguchi, United States
    - Pair skating champions: Natalia Mishkutenok & Artur Dmitriev
    - Ice dancing champions: Marina Klimova & Sergei Ponomarenko

1993

- World Figure Skating Championships:
    - Men's champion: Kurt Browning, Canada
    - Ladies' champion: Oksana Baiul, Ukraine
    - Pairs' champions: Isabelle Brasseur & Lloyd Eisler, Canada
    - Ice dancing champions: Maya Usova & Alexander Zhulin, Russia

1994

- World Figure Skating Championships:
    - Men's champion: Elvis Stojko, Canada Ladies' champion: Yuka Sato, Japan Pairs' champions: Evgenia Shishkova and Vadim Naumov, Russia Ice dancing champions: Oksana Grishuk and Evgeny Platov, Russia

1995

- World Figure Skating Championships:
    - Men's champion: Elvis Stojko, Canada Ladies' champion: Lu Chen, China Pairs' champions: Radka Kovariková / Rene Novotny, Czech Republic Ice dancing champions: Oksana Grishuk / Evgeny Platov, Russia

1996

- World Figure Skating Championships:
    - Men's champion: Todd Eldredge, United States
    - Ladies' champion: Michelle Kwan, United States
    - Pairs' champions: Marina Eltsova / Sergei Bushkov, Russia
    - Ice dancing champions: Oksana Grishuk / Evgeny Platov, Russia

FIGURE SKATING

1997

- World Figure Skating Championships:
    - Men's champion: Elvis Stojko, Canada Ladies' champion: Tara Lipinski, United States Pairs' champions: Mandy Wötzel & Ingo Steuer, Germany Ice dancing champions: Oksana Grishuk / Evgeny Platov, Russia

1998

- World Figure Skating Championships:
    - Men's champion: Alexei Yagudin, Russia Ladies' champion: Michelle Kwan, United States Pairs' champions: Elena Bereschnaya / Anton Sicharulidze, Russia Ice dancing champions: Anjelika Krylova / Oleg Ovsyannikov, Russia

1999

- World Figure Skating Championships:
    - Men's champion: Alexei Yagudin, Russia Ladies' champion: Maria Butyrskaya, Russia Pairs' champions: Yelena Berezhnaya & Anton Sikharulidze, Russia Ice dancing champions: Anjelika Krylova & Oleg Ovsyannikov, Russia
- European Figure Skating Championships:
    - Men's champion: Alexei Yagudin, Russia Ladies' champion: Maria Butyrskaya, Russia Pairs' champions: Maria Petrova & Alexei Tikhonov, Russia Ice dancing champions: Anjelika Krylova & Oleg Ovsyannikov, Russia

2000

- World Figure Skating Championships:
    - Men's champion: Alexei Yagudin, Russia Ladies' champion: Michelle Kwan, United States Pairs' champions: Maria Petrova and Alexei Tikhonov, Russia Ice dance champions: Marina Anissina and Gwendal Peizerat, France

FOOTBALL

1950

- NFL Championship: Cleveland Browns win 30-28 over Los Angeles Rams
- Oklahomer Sooners– College football champions

1951

- January 14– The national football league has its first Pro Bowl game (Los Angeles California)
- NFL Championship: Los Angeles Rams won 24-17 over the Cleveland Browns

1952

- NFL Championship: Detroit lions won 17-7 over Cleveland Browns
  Oklahomer Sooners– College football champions

1953

- NFL Championship: Detroit lions won 17-16 over Cleveland Browns

1954

- NFL Championship: Cleveland Browns won 38-14 over the Los Angeles Rams
- Oklahomer Sooners– College football champions

1955

- November 12: College football: Ucla narrowly defeated Washington 19-17; Michigan State crushed Minnesota 42-14; Ohio State beat Iowa 20-10; Michigan blanked Indiana 30-0; It was Notre Dame over North Carolina 27-7; Oklahomer ripped Iowa State 52-0; West Virginia lost to Pittsburgh 26-7; Texas A&M over Rice 20-10; Maryland defeated Clemson 25-12; And it was Texas Christian over Texas 47-20

1956

- NFL Championship: New York Giants won 47-7 over Chicago Bears
- Oklahomer Sooners– College football champions

1957

- NFL Championship: Detroit lions won 59-14 over Cleveland Browns

FOOTBALL

1958

- NFL Championship: December 28 the Baltimore Colts won 23-17 over the New York Giants in overtime. The game is later called the "Greatest game ever played".
- College football: Louisiana State University wins their first recognized national championship in the poll era. See 1958 LSU Tigers football team.

1959

- NFL Championship: Baltimore Colts won 31-16 over the New York Giants

1960

- Minnesota Golden Gophers win National college football championship.
- National Football League names Pete Rozelle commissioner of the league. The league expands to Dallas for the 1960 season and Minneapolis-St.Paul for the 1961 season. The Chicago Cardinals relocates to St. Louis, Missouri.
- December 26-NFL Championship: Philadelphia Eagles won 17-13 over the Green Bay Packers
- The American Football League (AFL) played its first season
- First black pro football placekicker: Gene Mingo (Denver Broncos, AFL)
- First Hispanic pro football quarterback: Tom Flores (Oakland Raiders, AFL)
- AFL Championship: Houston Oilers won 24-16 over the Los Angeles Chargers

1961

- AFL Championship: Houston Oilers won 10-3 over the San Diego Chargers
- NFL Championship: Green Bay Packers won 37-0 over the New York Giants
- NCAA I-A Championship:
  - University of Alabama (AP)(UPI)
  - Ohio State (FWAA)

1962

- AFL Championship: Dallas Texans won 20-17 over the Houston Oilers in double overtime
- NFL Championship: Green Bay Packers won 16-7 over the New York Giants

1963

- January 29 - First inductees into the Pro Football Hall of Fame are announced
- AFL Eastern Division Playoff: Boston Patriots win 26-8 over the Buffalo Bills
- AFL Championship: San Diego Chargers win 51-10 over the Boston Patriots
- NFL Championship: Chicago Bears win 14-10 over the New York Giants
- September 7 - The Pro Football Hall of Fame opens in Canton, Ohio with 17 charter members.
- The Heisman Trophy: Roger Staubach, Navy

FOOTBALL

1964

- AFL Championship:1964 - Buffalo Bills win 11-7 over the San Diego Chargers
- NFL Championship:December 1964 - Cleveland Browns win 27-0 over the Baltimore Colts

1965

- AFL Championship Buffalo Bills won 23-0 over the San Diego Chargers
- NFL Championship: Green Bay Packers won 23-12 over the Cleveland Browns

1966

- 1966 season championships were played in late 1966 and early 1967
- AFL Championship: Kansas City Chiefs won 31-7 over the Buffalo Bills
- NFL Championship: Green Bay Packers won 34-27 over the Dallas Cowboys
- Super Bowl I: Green Bay Packers won 35-10 over the Kansas City Chiefs

1967

- The first Super Bowl is played on January 15: The NFL champion Green Bay Packers win 35-10 over the AFL champion Kansas City Chiefs. This was following the 1966 season.
- On December 31, the Green Bay Packers defeat the Dallas Cowboys 21-17 for the 1967 NFL Championship in a now-legendary game at Lambeau Field known as the Ice Bowl.
- Oakland Raiders defeat the Houston Oilers 40-7 for the 1967 American Football League Championship.

1968

- January 14 Super Bowl II: Green Bay Packers won 33-14 over the Oakland Raiders
- November 17: The Oakland Raiders score two consecutive touchdowns in the last minute of the fourth quarter to beat the New York Jets 43-32, in the infamous "Heidi Game".
- Baltimore Colts 34-0 Cleveland Browns in 1968 NFL championship game.
- New York Jets 27-23 Oakland Raiders in the 1968 AFL championship game.

1969

- January 12 - The American Football League New York Jets upset the NFL's heavily favored Baltimore Colts in Super Bowl III by a score of 16-7, after quarterback Joe Namath "guaranteed" a victory.
- September 28 - Minnesota Vikings' Quarterback Joe Kapp became the last player to throw seven touchdowns in a single game.
- Kansas City Chiefs 17-7 Oakland Raiders for 1969 AFL championship.
- Minnesota Vikings 27-7 Cleveland Browns for the 1969 NFL championship.

FOOTBALL

1970

- Super Bowl IV: Kansas City Chiefs won 23-7 over the Minnesota Vikings
- Nebraska Cornhuskers win the college football national championship.
- November 14: A plane carrying most of the Marshall University team crashes just short of landing near Huntington, West Virginia, killing all 75 aboard, including 37 players.

1971

- Super Bowl V: Baltimore Colts won 16-13 over the Dallas Cowboys
- December 25 - The Miami Dolphins defeat the Kansas City Chiefs in a divisional playoff game. The double-overtime contest is the longest game in NFL history, and the Chiefs' last-ever home game at Municipal Stadium.
- 1970 NCAA Division I-A national football championship: The Nebraska Cornhuskers win 17-12 over the LSU Tigers on January 1, 1971.

1972

- January 16-Super Bowl VI: Dallas Cowboys won 24-3 over the Miami Dolphins
- 1971 NCAA Division I-A national football championship: The Nebraska Cornhuskers win 38-6 over the University of Alabama Crimson Tide to claim back-to-back National Championship titles on January 1, 1972.

1973

- O.J. Simpson becomes the first player in NFL history to rush for more than 2,000 yards in a single season.
- Super Bowl VII: Miami Dolphins won 14-7 over the Washington Redskins to complete the only unbeaten NFL season

1974

- Super Bowl VIII: The Miami Dolphins won 24-7 over the Minnesota Vikings
- Oklahoma Sooners - college football championship.

1975

- Super Bowl IX: Pittsburgh Steelers won 16-6 over the Minnesota Vikings
- Oklahoma Sooners - college football championship.

1976

- Super Bowl X: January 18 Pittsburgh Steelers won 21-17 over the Dallas Cowboys
- Pittsburgh Panthers are voted NCAA Football National Champions.

FOOTBALL

1970

- Super Bowl IV: Kansas City Chiefs won 23-7 over the Minnesota Vikings
- Nebraska Cornhuskers win the college football national championship.
- November 14: A plane carrying most of the Marshall University team crashes just short of landing near Huntington, West Virginia, killing all 75 aboard, including 37 players.

1971

- Super Bowl V: Baltimore Colts won 16-13 over the Dallas Cowboys
- December 25 - The Miami Dolphins defeat the Kansas City Chiefs in a divisional playoff game. The double-overtime contest is the longest game in NFL history, and the Chiefs' last-ever home game at Municipal Stadium.
- 1970 NCAA Division I-A national football championship: The Nebraska Cornhuskers win 17-12 over the LSU Tigers on January 1, 1971.

1972

- January 16-Super Bowl VI: Dallas Cowboys won 24-3 over the Miami Dolphins
- 1971 NCAA Division I-A national football championship: The Nebraska Cornhuskers win 38-6 over the University of Alabama Crimson Tide to claim back-to-back National Championship titles on January 1, 1972.

1973

- O.J. Simpson becomes the first player in NFL history to rush for more than 2,000 yards in a single season.
- Super Bowl VII: Miami Dolphins won 14-7 over the Washington Redskins to complete the only unbeaten NFL season

1974

- Super Bowl VIII: The Miami Dolphins won 24-7 over the Minnesota Vikings
- Oklahoma Sooners - college football championship

1975

- Super Bowl IX: Pittsburgh Steelers won 16-6 over the Minnesota Vikings
- Oklahoma Sooners - college football championship.

1976

- Super Bowl X: January 18 Pittsburgh Steelers won 21-17 over the Dallas Cowboys
- Pittsburgh Panthers are voted NCAA Football National Champions.

FOOTBALL

1977

- Super Bowl XI: Oakland Raiders won 32-14 over the Minnesota Vikings

1978

- Super Bowl XII: Dallas Cowboys won 27-10 over the Denver Broncos

1979

- January 21 - Super Bowl XIII: Pittsburgh Steelers won 35-31 over the Dallas Cowboys

1980

- Super Bowl XIV: Pittsburgh Steelers won 31-19 over the Los Angeles Rams

1981

- January 25 - Super Bowl XV: Oakland Raiders won 27-10 over the Philadelphia Eagles

1982

- Super Bowl XVI: San Francisco 49ers won 26-21 over the Cincinnati Bengals
- NCAA Division I-A: Clemson University Tigers defeat University of Nebraska Cornhuskers 22-15 in the Orange Bowl, voted 1981 NCAA Division I-A College Football National Champion in AP and UPI polls.
- Strike: First regular season strike by NFL players ends on November 16 after 57 days.

1983

- Super Bowl XVII: Washington Redskins won their first Super Bowl title, and first NFL title since 1942, 27-17 over the Miami Dolphins.
- The Miami Hurricanes win their first national championship over the Nebraska Cornhuskers 31-30 in the Orange Bowl.

1984

- Super Bowl XVIII: Los Angeles Raiders won 38-9 over the Washington Redskins
- Walter Payton breaks Jim Brown's rushing record on October 7th.
- Brigham Young University, or (BYU) wins NCAA National Championship

FOOTBALL

1985

- January 20 Super Bowl XIX: San Francisco 49ers won 38-16 over the Miami Dolphins
- Oklahoma Sooners - college football championship.

1986

- January 26 - Super Bowl XX: Chicago Bears won 46-10 over the New England Patriots

1987

- Super Bowl XXI: New York Giants won 39-20 over the Denver Broncos

1988

- Super Bowl XXII: Washington Redskins win their second Super Bowl title and fourth NFL title 42-10 over the Denver Broncos.
- Notre Dame Fighting Irish defeat West Virginia Mountaineers in college National Championship game.

1989

- Super Bowl XXIII: San Francisco 49ers won 20-16 over the Cincinnati Bengals

1990

- January 28 - Super Bowl XXIV - San Francisco 49ers won 55-10 over the Denver Broncos

1991

- Super Bowl XXV: New York Giants won 20-19 over the Buffalo Bills
- World Bowl '91: London Monarchs won 21-0 over the Barcelona Dragons in the inaugural World Bowl.

1992

- Super Bowl XXVI: Washington Redskins won 37-24 over the Buffalo Bills
- November 29 - Dennis Byrd of the New York Jets is paralyzed from a neck injury during an NFL game against the Kansas City Chiefs. He made a recovery that bordered on the miraculous; although he would never play again, he would walk unassisted several months later.

FOOTBALL

1993

- Super Bowl XXVII: Dallas Cowboys won 52-17 over the Buffalo Bills

1994

- Super Bowl XXVIII: Dallas Cowboys won 30-13 over the Buffalo Bills

1995

- Super Bowl XXIX: San Francisco 49ers won 49-26 over the San Diego Chargers.
- 1994 NCAA Division I-A national football championship: The Nebraska Cornhuskers defeat the University of Miami Hurricanes 24-17 on January 1, 1995.
- The World League of American Football is resumed after 2 years without play. Frankfurt Galaxy win the World Bowl 26-22 over the Amsterdam Admirals.

1996

- Super Bowl XXX: Dallas Cowboys won 27-17 over the Pittsburgh Steelers
- 1995 NCAA Division I-A national football championship: the Nebraska Cornhuskers manhandle the University of Florida Gators, winning 62-24, along with their second back-to-back National Championship seasons on January 2, 1996.
- World Bowl 96: The Scottish Claymores won 32-27 over the Frankfurt Galaxy.

1997

- Super Bowl XXXI: Green Bay Packers won 35-21 over the New England Patriots
- Florida Gators stomp Florida State Seminoles and win their first national title in college football.

1998

- January 13 - ABC and ESPN negotiate a $1.15 billion a season contract to keep Monday Night Football.
- Super Bowl XXXII: Denver Broncos won 31-24 over the Green Bay Packers
- NCAA: BCS National Championship (Fiesta Bowl): Tennessee Volunteers (13-0) won 23-16 over the Florida State Seminoles (11-2)

FOOTBALL

1999

- Sugar Bowl: The Florida State Seminoles won 49-29 over the Virginia Tech Hokies in the Bowl Championship Series National Championship Game.
- Super Bowl XXXIII: Denver Broncos won 34-19 over the Atlanta Falcons

2000

- Super Bowl XXXIV: Saint Louis Rams win 23-16 over the Tennessee Titans
- Marshall Faulk wins the regular season MVP award.
- Oklahoma Sooners - college football championship.

GOLF

1950

- Men's Golf
- Grand Slam of golf results:
  - May - The Masters - Jimmy Demaret
  - June - US Open - Ben Hogan
  - July - British Open - Bobby Locke
  - August - PGA Championship - Chandler Harper
    - PGA tour's leading money winner for the year: Sam Snead - $35,759
- Women's Golf
  - Babe Zaharias named Woman Athlete of the Half-Century by the Associated Press.
  - US Women's Open - Babe Zaharias
  - Thirteen women golfers found the Ladies Professional Golf Association (LPGA).

1951

- Men's Golf
- Grand Slam of golf results:
  - May - The Masters - Ben Hogan
  - June - US Open - Ben Hogan
  - July - British Open - Max Faulkner
  - August - PGA Championship - Sam Snead
- PGA tour's leading money winner for the year: Lloyd Mangrum - $26,089
- Ryder Cup: United States team wins 9 1/2 to 2 1/2 over the British team in world golf.
- Women's Golf
- US Women's Open - Betsy Rawls

1952

- Men's Golf
- Grand Slam of golf results:
  - April - The Masters - Sam Snead
  - June - US Open - Julius Boros
  - July - British Open - Bobby Locke
  - August - PGA Championship - Jim Turnesa
- PGA tour's leading money winner for the year: Julius Boros - $37,033
- Women's Golf
- US Women's Open - Louise Suggs

GOLF

1953

- Men's Golf
- Grand Slam of golf results:
    - May - The Masters - Ben Hogan
    - June - US Open - Ben Hogan
    - July - British Open - Ben Hogan
    - August - PGA Championship - Walter Burkemo
- PGA tour's leading money winner for the year: Lew Worsham - $34,002
- Ryder Cup: United States wins 6 1/2 to 5 1/2 over the British team in world golf.
- Women's Golf
- The US Women's Open - Betsy Rawls

1954

- Men's Golf
- Grand Slam of golf results:
    - April - The Masters - Sam Snead
    - June - US Open - Ed Furgol
    - July - The Open Championship - Peter Thomson
    - August - PGA Championship - Chick Harbert
- PGA tour's leading money winner for the year: Bob Toski - $65,820
- Women's Golf
- US Women's Open - Babe Zaharias
- Patty Berg: leading money winner on the LPGA tour, earning $16,011.

1955

- Men's Golf
- Grand Slam of golf results:
    - April - The Masters - Cary Middlecoff
    - June - US Open - Jack Fleck
    - July - British Open - Peter Thomson
    - August - PGA Championship - Doug Ford
- PGA tour's leading money winner for the year: Julius Boros - $63,122
- Ryder Cup the United States team wins 8-4 over the British team in world golf.
- Women's Golf
- The LPGA launches the new LPGA Championship annual tournament.
- US Women's Open - Fay Crocker
- LPGA Championship - Beverly Hanson
- Patty Berg: leading money winner on the LPGA tour, earning $16,492.

GOLF

1956

- Men's golf
- Grand Slam of golf results:
    - May - The Masters - Jack Burke, Jr.
    - June - US Open - Cary Middlecoff
    - July - British Open - Peter Thomson
    - August - PGA Championship - Jack Burke
- PGA tour's leading money winner for the year: Ted Kroll - $72,836
- Women's golf
- US Women's Open - Kathy Cornelius
- LPGA Championship - Marlene Hagge
- Marlene Hagge: leading money winner on the LPGA tour, earning $20,235.

1957

- Men's Golf
- Grand Slam of golf results:
    - May - The Masters - Doug Ford
    - June - US Open - Dick Mayer
    - July - British Open - Bobby Locke
    - August - PGA Championship - Lionel Hebert
- PGA tour's leading money winner for the year: Dick Mayer - $65,835
- Ryder Cup: Britain wins 7 1/2 to 4 1/2 over the United States in world team golf.
- Women's Golf
- US Women's Open - Betsy Rawls
- LPGA Championship - Louise Suggs
- Patty Berg: leading money winner on the LPGA tour, earning $16,272.

1958

- Men's Golf
- Grand Slam of golf results:
    - April 6 - The Masters golf tournament - Arnold Palmer
    - June - US Open - Tommy Bolt
    - July - British Open - Bobby Locke
    - August - PGA Championship - Dow Finsterwald
- PGA tour's leading money winner for the year: Arnold Palmer - $42,608
- Women's Golf
- US Women's Open - Mickey Wright
- LPGA Championship - Mickey Wright
- Beverly Hanson: leading money winner on the LPGA tour, earning $12,629.

GOLF

1959

- Men's golf
- Grand Slam of golf results:
    - May — The Masters golf tournament — Art Wall, Jr.
    - June — US Open — Billy Casper
    - July — British Open — Gary Player
    - August — PGA Championship — Bob Rosburg
- PGA tour's leading money winner for the year: Art Wall, Jr. — $53,168
- Ryder Cup: United States 8½ to 3½ over Britain in world team golf
- Women's golf
- US Women's Open — Mickey Wright
- LPGA Championship — Betsy Rawls
- Betsy Rawls: leading money winner on the LPGA tour, earning $26,774.

1960

- Men's Golf
- Grand Slam of golf results:
    - April 10 - The Masters - Arnold Palmer
    - June - US Open - Arnold Palmer
    - July - British Open - Kel Nagle
    - August - PGA Championship - Jay Hebert
- PGA tour's leading money winner for the year: Arnold Palmer - $75,263
- Women's Golf
- US Women's Open - Betsy Rawls
- LPGA Championship - Mickey Wright
- Louise Suggs: leading money winner on the LPGA tour, earning $16,892

1961

- Men's Golf
- Grand Slam of golf results:
    - April - The Masters - Gary Player _ Player became the first international golfer to win The Masters.
    - June - US Open - Gene Littler
    - July - British Open - Arnold Palmer
    - August - PGA Championship - Jerry Barber
- PGA tour's leading money winner for the year: Gary Player - $64,540
- Ryder Cup: United States wins 14 1/2 to 9 1/2 over Britain in world team golf.
- Women's Golf
- US Women's Open - Mickey Wright
- LPGA Championship - Mickey Wright
- Mickey Wright: leading money winner on the LPGA tour, earning $22,236

GOLF

1962

- Men's Golf
- Grand Slam of golf results:
    - May - The Masters golf tournament - Arnold Palmer
    - June - US Open - Jack Nicklaus
    - July - British Open - Arnold Palmer
    - August - PGA Championship - Gary Player
- PGA tour's leading money winner for the year: Arnold Palmer - $81,448
- Women's Golf
- US Women's Open - Murle Lindstrom
- LPGA Championship - Judy Kimball
- Mickey Wright: leading money winner on the LPGA tour, earning $21,641

1963

- Men's Golf
- Grand Slam of golf results:
    - May - The Masters - Jack Nicklaus
    - June - US Open - Julius Boros
    - July - British Open - Bob Charles
    - August - PGA Championship - Jack Nicklaus
- PGA tour's leading money winner for the year: Arnold Palmer - $128,230
- Ryder Cup: United States wins 23 to 9 over Britain in world team golf.
- Women's Golf
- US Women's Open - Mary Mills
- LPGA Championship - Mickey Wright
- Mickey Wright: leading money winner on the LPGA tour, earning $31,269

1964

- Men's Golf
- Grand Slam of golf results:
    - April 12 - The Masters - Arnold Palmer
    - June - US Open - Ken Venturi
    - July - British Open - Tony Lema
    - August - PGA Championship - Bobby Nichols
- PGA tour's leading money winner for the year: Jack Nicklaus - $113,285
- Women's Golf
- US Women's Open - Mickey Wright
- LPGA Championship - Mary Mills
- Mickey Wright: leading money winner on the LPGA tour, earning $29,800

GOLF

1965

- Men's Golf
- Grand Slam of golf results:
    - May - The Masters - Jack Nicklaus
    - June - US Open - Gary Player
    - July - British Open - Peter Thomson
    - August - PGA Championship - Dave Marr
- PGA tour's leading money winner for the year: Jack Nicklaus - $140,752
- Ryder Cup: United States wins 19½ to 12½ over Britain in world team golf.
- Women's Golf
- US Women's Open - Carol Mann
- LPGA Championship - Sandra Haynie
- Kathy Whitworth: leading money winner on the LPGA tour, earning $28,658

1966

- Men's Golf
- Grand Slam of golf results:
    - May - The Masters golf tournament - Jack Nicklaus
    - June - US Open - Billy Casper
    - July - British Open - Jack Nicklaus
    - August - PGA Championship - Al Geiberger
- PGA tour's leading money winner for the year: Billy Casper - $121,945
- Women's Golf
- US Women's Open - Sandra Spuzich
- LPGA Championship - Gloria Ehret
- Kathy Whitworth: leading money winner on the LPGA tour, earning $33,517.

1967

- Men's Golf
- Grand Slam of golf results:
    - April — The Masters — Gay Brewer
    - June — US Open — Jack Nicklaus
    - July — British Open — Roberto De Vicenzo
    - August — PGA Championship — Don January
- PGA tour's leading money winner for the year: Jack Nicklaus — $188,998
- Ryder Cup: United States wins 23½ to 8½ over Britain in world team golf.
- Women's Golf
- US Women's Open — Catherine Lacoste
- LPGA Championship — Kathy Whitworth
- Kathy Whitworth: leading money winner on the LPGA tour, earning $32,937.

GOLF

1968

- Men's Golf
- Grand Slam of golf results:
    - May - The Masters - Bob Goalby
    - June - US Open - Lee Trevino
    - July - British Open - Gary Player
    - August - PGA Championship - Julius Boros
- PGA tour's leading money winner for the year: Billy Casper - $205,169
- Women's Golf
- Canadian rookie Sandra Post became the youngest golfer, male or female, to ever win a PGA TOUR major tournament by capturing the LPGA Championship.
- US Women's Open - Susie Berning
- LPGA Championship: Sandra Post
- Kathy Whitworth: leading money winner on the LPGA tour, earning $48,379

1969

- Men's Golf
- Grand Slam of golf results:
    - May - The Masters - George Archer
    - June - US Open - Orville Moody
    - July - British Open - Tony Jacklin
    - August - PGA Championship - Ray Floyd
- PGA tour's leading money winner for the year: Frank Beard - $164,707
- Ryder Cup: United States and Britain tied 16 all in world team golf.
- Women's Golf
- US Women's Open - Donna Caponi
- LPGA Championship - Betsy Rawls
- Carol Mann: leading money winner on the LPGA tour, earning $49,152.

1970

- Men's Golf
- Grand Slam of golf results:
    - May - The Masters - Billy Casper
    - June - US Open - Tony Jacklin
    - July - British Open - Jack Nicklaus
    - August - PGA Championship - Dave Stockton
- PGA tour's leading money winner for the year: Lee Trevino - $157,037
- Women's Golf
- US Open - Donna Caponi
- LPGA Championship - Shirley Englehorn
- Kathy Whitworth: leading money winner on the LPGA tour, earning $30,235

GOLF

1971

- Men's Golf
- Grand Slam of golf results:
    - May - The Masters - Charles Coody
    - June - US Open - Lee Trevino
    - July - British Open - Lee Trevino
    - August - PGA Championship - Jack Nicklaus
- PGA tour's leading money winner for the year: Jack Nicklaus - $244,491
- Ryder Cup: United States won 18 1/2 to 13 1/2 over Britain in world team golf
- Women's Golf
- US Women's Open - JoAnne Carner
- LPGA Championship - Kathy Whitworth
- Kathy Whitworth: leading money winner on the LPGA tour, earning $41,181

1972

- Men's Golf
- The European Tour begins its first season of competition.
- Grand Slam of golf results:
    - April - The Masters - Jack Nicklaus
    - June - US Open - Jack Nicklaus
    - July - The Open Championship - Lee Trevino
    - August - PGA Championship - Gary Player
- PGA Tour leading money winner for the year: Jack Nicklaus - $320,542
- Women's Golf
- US Women's Open - Susie Berning
- LPGA Championship - Kathy Ahern
- Kathy Whitworth: leading money winner on the LPGA tour, earning $65,063

1973

- Men's Golf
- Major Championship results:
    - May - The Masters - Tommy Aaron
    - June - US Open - Johnny Miller
    - July - British Open - Tom Weiskopf
    - August - PGA Championship - Jack Nicklaus
- PGA tour's leading money winner for the year: Jack Nicklaus - $308,362
- Ryder Cup: United States won 19-13 over Britain & Ireland in world team golf.
- Women's Golf
- US Women's Open - Susie Berning
- LPGA Championship - Mary Mills
- Kathy Whitworth: leading money winner on the LPGA tour, earning $82,854

GOLF

1974

- Men's Golf
- Grand Slam of golf results:
    - May - The Masters - Gary Player
    - June - US Open - Hale Irwin
    - July - British Open - Gary Player
    - August - PGA Championship - Lee Trevino
- PGA tour's leading money winner for the year: Johnny Miller - $353,022
- Women's Golf
- US Women's Open - Sandra Haynie
- LPGA Championship - Sandra Haynie
- JoAnne Carner: leading money winner on the LPGA tour, earning $87,094.

1975

- Men's Golf
- Grand Slam of golf results:
    - May - The Masters - Jack Nicklaus
    - June - US Open - Lou Graham
    - July - British Open - Tom Watson
    - August - PGA Championship - Jack Nicklaus
- PGA tour's leading money winner for the year: Jack Nicklaus - $298,149
- Ryder Cup: United States wins 21-11 over Britain & Ireland in world team golf
- Women's Golf
- US Women's Open - Sandra Palmer
- LPGA Championship - Kathy Whitworth
- Sandra Palmer is the leading money winner on the LPGA tour with earnings of $94,805.

1976

- Men's Golf
- Grand Slam of golf results:
    - May - The Masters - Ray Floyd
    - June - US Open - Jerry Pate
    - July - British Open - Johnny Miller
    - August - PGA Championship - Dave Stockton
- PGA tour's leading money winner for the year: Jack Nicklaus - $266,439
- Women's Golf
- US Women's Open - JoAnne Carner
- LPGA Championship - Betty Burfeindt
- Judy Rankin is the leading money winner on the LPGA tour. With total earnings of $150,734, she is the first to ever earn more than $100,000 in a season.

GOLF

1977

- Men's Golf
- Grand Slam of golf results:
    - May - The Masters - Tom Watson
    - June - US Open - Hubert Green
    - July - British Open - Tom Watson
    - August - PGA Championship - Lanny Wadkins
- PGA tour's leading money winner for the year: Tom Watson - $310,653
- Ryder Cup: United States won 12½ -7½ over Britain & Ireland in world team golf. This was the last Ryder Cup to feature a side exclusively from the British Isles; the U.S. opponents in the next Ryder Cup, held in 1979 at White Sulphur Springs, West Virginia, would be drawn from all of Europe. The U.S.-Europe format has continued ever since.
- Women's Golf
- US Women's Open - Hollis Stacy
- LPGA Championship - Chako Higuchi
- Judy Rankin: leading money winner on the LPGA tour, earning $122,890.

1978

- Men's golf
- Grand Slam of golf results:
    - May - The Masters - Gary Player
    - June - US Open - Andy North
    - July - British Open - Jack Nicklaus
    - August - PGA Championship - John Mahaffey
- PGA tour's leading money winner for the year: Tom Watson - $362,429
- Women's golf
- US Women's Open - Hollis Stacy
- LPGA Championship - Nancy Lopez
- Nancy Lopez: leading money winner on the LPGA tour, earning $189,213.

1979

- Men's Golf
- Grand Slam of golf results:
    - April - The Masters - Fuzzy Zoeller. Zoeller defeated Ed Sneed and Tom Watson in the second hole of a sudden-death playoff, the first time this method was used.
    - June - US Open - Hale Irwin
    - July 20 - British Open - Seve Ballesteros. He becomes the first golfer from Continental Europe to win a major since Arnaud Massy of France won this in 1907.
    - August - PGA Championship - David Graham
- PGA tour's leading money winner for the year: Tom Watson - $462,636
- Ryder Cup: United States won 17-11 over Europe in the first Ryder Cup to feature a side representing all Europe.
- Women's Golf
- US Women's Open - Jerilyn Britz
- LPGA Championship - Donna Caponi
- Nancy Lopez: leading money winner on the LPGA tour, earning $189,213.

GOLF

1980

- Men's Golf
- January - the Senior PGA Tour (*Champions Tour*) is founded.
- Major championship results:
    - May - The Masters - Seve Ballesteros
    - June - US Open - Jack Nicklaus
    - July - British Open - Tom Watson
    - August - PGA Championship - Jack Nicklaus
- PGA Tour leading money winner for the year: Tom Watson - $530,808
- Champions Tour - In its first year, Don January is the leading money winner earning $44,100.
- Women's Golf
- US Women's Open - Amy Alcott
- LPGA Championship - Sally Little
- Beth Daniel: leading money winner on the LPGA tour, earning $231,000.

1981

- Men's Golf
- Major championship results:
    - April - The Masters - Tom Watson
    - June - US Open - David Graham
    - July - British Open - Bill Rogers
    - August - PGA Championship - Larry Nelson
- PGA Tour leading money winner for the year: Tom Kite - $375,699
- Champions Tour leading money winner: Miller Barber - $83,136
- Ryder Cup: United States won 18 1/2 to 9 1/2 over Europe in world team golf.
- Women's Golf
- US Women's Open - Pat Bradley
- LPGA Championship - Donna Caponi
- Beth Daniel: leading money winner on the LPGA tour, earning $206,977.

1982

- Men's Golf
- Major championship results:
    - May - The Masters - Craig Stadler
    - June - US Open - Tom Watson
    - July - British Open - Tom Watson
    - August - PGA Championship - Ray Floyd
- PGA Tour leading money winner for the year: Craig Stadler - $446,462
- Champions Tour leading money winner: Miller Barber - $106,890
- Women's Golf
- US Women's Open - Janet Anderson
- LPGA Championship - Jan Stephenson
- JoAnne Carner: leading money winner on the LPGA tour, earning $310,399.

GOLF

1983

- Men's Golf
- Major championship results:
    - April - The Masters - Seve Ballesteros
    - June - US Open - Larry Nelson
    - July - British Open - Tom Watson
    - August - PGA Championship - Hal Sutton
- PGA Tour leading money winner for the year: Hal Sutton - $426,668
- Champions Tour leading money winner: Don January - $237,571
- Ryder Cup: United States won 14 1/2 - 13 1/2 over Europe in world team golf.
- Women's Golf
- US Women's Open - Jan Stephenson
- LPGA Championship - Patty Sheehan
- JoAnne Carner: leading money winner on the LPGA tour, earning $291,404.

1984

- Men's Golf
- Major championship results:
    - May 1 - The Masters - Ben Crenshaw
    - June 1 - US Open - Fuzzy Zoeller
    - July - British Open - Seve Ballesteros
    - August 1 - PGA Championship - Lee Trevino
- PGA Tour leading money winner for the year: Tom Watson - $476,260
- Champions Tour leading money winner: Don January - $328,597
- Women's Golf
- US Women's Open - Hollis Stacy
- LPGA Championship - Patty Sheehan
- Betsy King: leading money winner on the LPGA tour, earning $266,771

1985

- Men's Golf
- Major championship results:
    - April - The Masters - Bernhard Langer
    - June - US Open - Andy North
    - July - British Open - Sandy Lyle
    - August - PGA Championship - Hubert Green
- PGA Tour leading money winner for the year: Curtis Strange - $542,321
- Champions Tour leading money winner: Peter Thomson - $386,724
- Ryder Cup: Europe won 16 1/2 to 11 1/2 over the USA in world team golf
- Women's Golf
- US Women's Open - Kathy Baker
- LPGA Championship - Nancy Lopez
- Nancy Lopez: leading money winner on the LPGA tour, earning $416,472

GOLF

1986

- Men's Golf
- Major championship results:
  - April - The Masters - Jack Nicklaus
  - June - US Open - Ray Floyd
  - July - British Open - Greg Norman
  - August - PGA Championship - Bob Tway
- PGA Tour leading money winner for the year: Greg Norman - $653,296
- Champions Tour leading money winner: Bruce Crampton - $454,299
- Women's Golf
- US Women's Open - Jane Geddes
- LPGA Championship - Pat Bradley
- Pat Bradley: leading money winner on the LPGA tour, earning $492,021

1987

- Men's Golf
- Major championship results:
  - May - The Masters - Larry Mize
  - June - US Open - Scott Simpson
  - July - British Open - Nick Faldo
  - August - PGA Championship - Larry Nelson
- PGA Tour leading money winner for the year: Curtis Strange - $925,941
- Champions Tour leading money winner Chi Chi Rodriguez - $509,145
- Ryder Cup: Europe won 15-13 over the United States in world team golf.
- Women's Golf
- US Women's Open - Laura Davies
- LPGA Championship - Jane Geddes
- British Women's Open - Alison Nicholas
- Ayako Okamoto: leading money winner on the LPGA tour, earning $466,034

1988

- Men's Golf
- Major championship results:
  - May - The Masters - Sandy Lyle
  - June - US Open - Curtis Strange
  - July - British Open - Seve Ballesteros
  - August - PGA Championship - Jeff Sluman
- Professional Tour leading money winner for the year: Curtis Strange - $1,147,644
- Champions Tour leading money winner: Bob Charles - $533,929
- Women's Golf
- US Women's Open - Liselotte Neumann
- LPGA Championship - Sherri Turner
- Sherri Turner: leading money winner on the LPGA tour with earnings of $347,255.

GOLF

1989

- Men's Golf
- Major championship results:
    - April - The Masters - Nick Faldo
    - June - US Open - Curtis Strange
    - July - British Open - Mark Calcavecchia
    - August - PGA Championship - Payne Stewart
- PGA Tour leading money winner for the year: Tom Kite - $1,395,278
- Champions Tour leading money winner: Bob Charles - $725,887
- Ryder Cup: Europe and the United States teams tied 14-14 in world golf.
- Women's Golf
- US Women's Open - Betsy King
- LPGA Championship - Nancy Lopez
- Betsy King: leading money winner on the LPGA tour, earning $654,132

1990

- Men's Golf
- Major championship results:
    - April - The Masters - Nick Faldo
    - June - US Open - Hale Irwin
    - July - British Open - Nick Faldo
    - August - PGA Championship - Wayne Grady
- PGA Tour leading money winner for the year: Greg Norman - $1,165,477
- Champions Tour leading money winner: Lee Trevino - $1,190,518
- Women's Golf
- US Women's Open: Betsy King
- LPGA Championship - Beth Daniel
- Beth Daniel: leading money winner on the LPGA tour, earning $863,578

1991

- Men's Golf
- Major championship results:
    - May - The Masters golf tournament - Ian Woosnam
    - June - US Open - Payne Stewart
    - July - British Open - Ian Baker-Finch
    - August - PGA Championship - John Daly
- PGA Tour leading money winner for the year: Corey Pavin - $979,430
- Champions Tour leading money winner: Mike Hill - $1,065,657
- Ryder Cup: United States team won 14 1/2 - 13 ½ over the European team in world golf.
- Women's Golf
- US Women's Open - Meg Mallon
- LPGA Championship - Meg Mallon
- Pat Bradley: leading money winner on the LPGA tour, earning $763,118.

GOLF

1992

- Men's Golf
- Major championship results:
    - May - The Masters - Fred Couples June - US Open - Tom Kite July - British Open - Nick Faldo August - PGA Championship - Nick Price
- PGA Tour leading money winner for the year: Fred Couples - $1,344,188
- Champions Tour leading money winner: Lee Trevino - $1,027,002
- Women's Golf
- US Women's Open: Patty Sheehan LPGA Championship - Betsy King Dottie Mochrie; leading money winner on the LPGA tour, earning $693,335

1993

- Men's Golf
- Major championship results:
    - May - The Masters - Bernhard Langer June - US Open - Lee Janzen July - British Open - Greg Norman August - PGA Championship - Paul Azinger
- PGA tour's leading money winner for the year: Nick Price - $1,478,557
- PGA Champions Tour leading money winner: Dave Stockton - $1,175,944
- Ryder Cup: United States team won 15-13 over the Europe team in world golf.
- Women's Golf
- US Women's Open - Lauri Merten LPGA Championship - Patty Sheehan Betsy King: leading money winner on the LPGA tour, earning $595,992.

1994

- Men's Golf
- Major championship results:
    - May - The Masters - José María Olazábal June - US Open - Ernie Els July - British Open - Nick Price August - PGA Championship - Nick Price
- PGA tour's leading money winner for the year: Nick Price - $1,499,927
- PGA Champions Tour leading money winner: Dave Stockton - $1,402,519
- Tiger Woods becomes the youngest man ever to win the U.S. Amateur, at age 18.
- Women's Golf
- US Women's Open - Patty Sheehan LPGA Championship - Laura Davies Laura Davies: leading money winner on the LPGA tour, earning $687,201.

GOLF

1995

- Men's golf
- Major championship results:
    - May - The Masters - Ben Crenshaw June - US Open - Corey Pavin July - British Open - John Daly August - PGA Championship - Steve Elkington
- PGA tour's leading money winner for the year: Greg Norman - $1,654,959
- PGA Champions Tour leading money winner: Jim Colbert - $1,444,386
- Ryder Cup: Europe won 14 1/2 to 13 1/2 over the United States in world team golf.
- Women's golf
- US Women's Open - Annika Sörenstam LPGA Championship - Kelly Robbins Annika Sörenstam: leading money winner on the LPGA tour, earning $666,533

1996

- Men's golf
- Major championship results:
    - May - The Masters - Nick Faldo June - US Open - Steve Jones July - British Open - Tom Lehman August - PGA Championship - Mark Brooks
- PGA tour's leading money winner for the year: Tom Lehman - $1,780,159
- PGA Champions Tour leading money winner: Jim Colbert - $1,627,890
- Tiger Woods became the first golfer to win three consecutive U.S. Amateur titles. This was the sixth consecutive year in which he won a USGA championship, one short of Bobby Jones' record of seven. In September, he turned professional. In the last five regular tournaments of the year on the PGA TOUR, his finishes were 5-3-1-3-1, placing him among the tour's top 30 money-winners for the year and thereby qualifying him for the season-ending TOUR Championship. Woods was named the PGA Tour Rookie of the Year.
- Women's golf
- US Women's Open - Annika Sörenstam
- LPGA Championship - Laura Davies
- Karrie Webb is the leading money winner on the LPGA tour with earnings of $1,002,000 becoming the first ever woman to earn more than a million dollars in one golf season.

1997

- Men's golf
- Major championship results:
    - April 13 - The Masters - Tiger Woods June - US Open - Ernie Els July - British Open - Justin Leonard August - PGA Championship - Davis Love III
- PGA Tour Player of the Year: Tiger Woods
- PGA Tour leading money winner: Tiger Woods - $2,066,833
- PGA Tour rookie of the year: Stewart Cink
- Senior PGA Tour leading money winner: Hale Irwin - $2,343,364
- Ryder Cup: Europe won 14 1/2-13 1/2 over the United States in world team golf.
- Women's golf
- US Women's Open - Alison Nicholas LPGA Championship - Christa Johnson Annika Sörenstam: leading money winner on the LPGA tour, earning $1,236,789.

GOLF

1998

- Men's golf
- Major championship results:
    - April - The Masters - Mark O'Meara June - US Open - Lee Janzen July - British Open - Mark O'Meara August - PGA Championship - Vijay Singh
- PGA Tour Player of the Year: Mark O'Meara
- PGA Tour leading money winner: David Duval - $2,591,031
- PGA Tour rookie of the year: Steve Flesch
- Senior PGA Tour leading money winner: Hale Irwin - $2,861,945
- Women's golf
- US Women's Open: Se Ri Pak LPGA Championship: Se Ri Pak Annika Sörenstam: leading money winner on the LPGA tour, earning $1,092,748

1999

- Men's Golf
- Major championship results:
    - April - The Masters - José María Olazábal June - US Open - Payne Stewart July - British Open - Paul Lawrie August - PGA Championship - Tiger Woods
- PGA Tour Player of the Year: Tiger Woods
- PGA Tour leading money winner: Tiger Woods - $6,616,585
- PGA Tour rookie of the year: Carlos Franco
- Senior PGA TOUR leading money winner: Bruce Fleisher - $2,515,705
- Ryder Cup: United States won 14 1/2 to 13 1/2 over Europe in world team golf.
- Women's Golf
- US Women's Open - Juli Inkster
- LPGA Championship - Juli Inkster
- Karrie Webb: leading money winner on the LPGA tour, earning $1,591,959

2000

- Men's golf
- Major championship results:
    - May - The Masters - Vijay Singh
    - June - US Open - Tiger Woods wins by 15 shots, a record for all majors, with a US Open to-par record score of -12
    - July - British Open - Tiger Woods becomes the fifth golfer in history to achieve the modern "career grand slam," and sets the to-par record for all majors (-19)
    - August - PGA Championship - Tiger Woods becomes the first golfer since Ben Hogan in 1953 to win 3 majors in a calendar year.
- PGA Tour Player of the Year: Tiger Woods
- PGA Tour leading money winner: Tiger Woods - $9,188,321
- PGA Tour rookie of the year: Michael Clark II
- Tiger Woods set or tied a total of 27 PGA Tour records during the year
- Senior PGA Tour leading money winner: Larry Nelson - $2,708,005
- Women's golf
- US Women's Open: Karrie Webb
- LPGA Championship: Juli Inkster
- Karrie Webb: leading money winner on the LPGA tour, earning $1,876,853.

HORSE RACING

1950

- The United States National Museum of Racing and Hall of Fame was founded in Saratoga Springs, New York.
- Australia - Melbourne Cup - Comic Court
- Canada - Queen's Plate - McGill
- France - Prix de l'Arc de Triomphe - Tantieme
- Ireland - Irish Derby Stakes - Dark Warrior
- English Triple Crown Races:
    - Two Thousand Guineas Stakes - Palestine
    - Epsom Derby - Galcador
    - St. Leger Stakes - Talma
- United States Triple Crown Races:
    - Kentucky Derby - Middleground
    - Preakness Stakes - Hill Prince
    - Belmont Stakes - Middleground

1951

- July 14 - Citation won his 32nd race, the Hollywood Gold Cup, becoming the first equine millionaire.
- Australia - Melbourne Cup - Delat
- Canada - Queen's Plate - Major Factor
- France - Prix de l'Arc de Triomphe - Tantieme
- Ireland - Irish Derby Stakes - Fraise du Bois
- English Triple Crown Races:
    1. Two Thousand Guineas Stakes - Ki Ming
    2. Epsom Derby - Arctic Prince
    3. St. Leger Stakes - Talma
- United States Triple Crown Races:
    1. Kentucky Derby - Count Turf
    2. Preakness Stakes - Bold
    3. Belmont Stakes - Counterpoint

1952

- Australia - Melbourne Cup - Dalray
- Canada - Queen's Plate - Epigram
- France - Prix de l'Arc de Triomphe - Nuccio
- Ireland - Irish Derby Stakes - Thirteen of Diamonds
- English Triple Crown Races:
    - Two Thousand Guineas Stakes - Thunderhead
    - Epsom Derby - Tulyar
    - St. Leger Stakes - Tulyar
- United States Triple Crown Races:
    - Kentucky Derby - Hill Gail
    - Preakness Stakes - Blue Man
    - Belmont Stakes - One Count

HORSE RACING

1953

- Australia - Melbourne Cup - Wodalla
- Canada - Queen's Plate - Canadiana
- France - Prix de l'Arc de Triomphe - La Sorellina
- Ireland - Irish Derby Stakes - Chamier
- English Triple Crown Races:
    - Two Thousand Guineas Stakes - Nearula
    - Epsom Derby - Pinza
    - St. Leger Stakes - Premonition
- United States Triple Crown Races:
    - Kentucky Derby - Dark Star
    - Preakness Stakes - Native Dancer
    - Belmont Stakes - Native Dancer

1954

- Australia - Melbourne Cup - Rising Fast
- Canada - Queen's Plate - Collisteo
- France - Prix de l'Arc de Triomphe - Sica Boy
- Ireland - Irish Derby Stakes - Zarathustra
- English Triple Crown Races:
    - Two Thousand Guineas Stakes - Darius
    - Epsom Derby - Never Say Die
    - St. Leger Stakes - Never Say Die
- United States Triple Crown Races:
    - Kentucky Derby - Determine
    - Preakness Stakes - Hasty Road
    - Belmont Stakes - High Gun

1955

- Australia - Melbourne Cup - Toparoa
- Canada - Queen's Plate - Ace Marine
- France - Prix de l'Arc de Triomphe - Ribot
- Ireland - Irish Derby Stakes - Panaslipper
- English Triple Crown Races:
    - Two Thousand Guineas Stakes - Our Babu
    - Epsom Derby - Phil Drake
    - St. Leger Stakes - Meld
- United States Triple Crown Races:
    - Kentucky Derby - Swaps
    - Preakness Stakes - Nashua
    - Belmont Stakes - Nashua

HORSE RACING

1956

- Australia - Melbourne Cup - Evening Peal
- Canada - Queen's Plate - Canadian Champ
- France - Prix de l'Arc de Triomphe - Ribot
- Ireland - Irish Derby Stakes - Talgo
- English Triple Crown races:
    - Two Thousand Guineas Stakes - Gilles de Retz
    - Epsom Derby - Lavandin
    - St. Leger Stakes - Cambremer
- United States Triple Crown races:
    - Kentucky Derby - Needles
    - Preakness Stakes - Fabius
    - Belmont Stakes - Needles

1957

- Australia - Melbourne Cup - Straight Draw
- Canada - Queen's Plate - Lyford Cay
- France - Prix de l'Arc de Triomphe - Oroso
- Ireland - Irish Derby Stakes - Ballymoss
- English Triple Crown Races:
    - Two Thousand Guineas Stakes - Crepello
    - Epsom Derby - Crepello
    - St. Leger Stakes - Ballymoss
- United States Triple Crown Races:
    - Kentucky Derby - Iron Liege
    - Preakness Stakes - Bold Ruler
    - Belmont Stakes - Gallant Man

1958

- Australia - Melbourne Cup - Baystone
- Canada - Queen's Plate - Caledon Beau
- France - Prix de l'Arc de Triomphe - Ballymoss
- Ireland - Irish Derby Stakes - Sindon
- English Triple Crown Races:
    - Two Thousand Guineas Stakes - Pall Mall
    - Epsom Derby - Hard Ridden
    - St. Leger Stakes - Alcide
- Tim Tam, who had won the Kentucky Derby and Preakness, fractured a sesamoid bone and lost his chance for the Triple Crown when he hobbled across the finish line in second place at the Belmont Stakes.
- United States Triple Crown Races:
    - Kentucky Derby - Tim Tam
    - Preakness Stakes - Tim Tam
    - Belmont Stakes - Cavan

HORSE RACING

1959

- Australia — Melbourne Cup — Macdougal
- Canada — Queen's Plate — New Providence
- France — Prix de l'Arc de Triomphe — Saint Crespin
- Ireland — Irish Derby Stakes — Fidalgo
- English Triple Crown races:
    - Two Thousand Guineas Stakes — Taboun
    - Epsom Derby — Parthia
    - St. Leger Stakes — Cantelo
- United States Triple Crown races:
    - Kentucky Derby — Tomy Lee
    - Preakness Stakes — Royal Orbit
    - Belmont Stakes — Sword Dancer

1960

- Australia - Melbourne Cup
- Canada - Queen's Plate
- France - Prix de l'Arc de Triomphe
- Ireland - Irish Derby Stakes - Chamour
- English Triple Crown Races:
    - Two Thousand Guineas Stakes
    - Epsom Derby
    - St. Leger Stakes
- United States Triple Crown Races:
    - Kentucky Derby - Venetian Way
    - Preakness Stakes - Bally Ache
    - Belmont Stakes - Celtic Ash

1961

- Australia - Melbourne Cup - Lord Fury
- Canada - Queen's Plate - Blue Light
- France - Prix de l'Arc de Triomphe - Molvedo
- Ireland - Irish Derby Stakes - Your Highness
- English Triple Crown Races:
    - Two Thousand Guineas Stakes - Rockavon
    - Epsom Derby - Psidium
    - St. Leger Stakes - Aurelius
- United States Triple Crown Races:
    - Kentucky Derby - Carry Back
    - Preakness Stakes - Carry Back
    - Belmont Stakes - Sherluck

HORSE RACING

1965

- Australia - Melbourne Cup - Light Fingers
- Canada - Queen's Plate - Whistling Sea
- France - Prix de l'Arc de Triomphe - Sea-Bird II
- Ireland - Irish Derby Stakes - Meadow Court
- English Triple Crown Races:
    - Two Thousand Guineas Stakes - Niksar
    - Epsom Derby - Sea-Bird
    - St. Leger Stakes - Provoke
- United States Triple Crown Races:
    - Kentucky Derby - Lucky Debonair
    - Preakness Stakes - Tom Rolfe
    - Belmont Stakes - Hail to All (Held at Aqueduct)

1966

- Australia - Melbourne Cup - Galilee
- Canada - Queen's Plate - Titled Hero
- France - Prix de l'Arc de Triomphe - Bon Mot III
- Ireland - Irish Derby Stakes - Sodium
- English Triple Crown Races:
    - Two Thousand Guineas Stakes - Kashmir
    - Epsom Derby - Charlottown
    - St. Leger Stakes - Sodium
- United States Triple Crown Races:
    - Kentucky Derby - Kauai King
    - Preakness Stakes - Kauai King
    - Belmont Stakes - Amberoid (Held at Aqueduct)

1967

- Australia — Melbourne Cup — Red Handed
- Canada — Queen's Plate — Jammed Lovely
- France — Prix de l'Arc de Triomphe — Topyo
- Ireland — Irish Derby Stakes — Ribocco
- English Triple Crown Races:
    - Two Thousand Guineas Stakes — Royal Palace
    - Epsom Derby — Royal Palace
    - St. Leger Stakes — Ribocco
- United States Triple Crown Races:
    - Kentucky Derby — Proud Clarion
    - Preakness Stakes — Damascus
    - Belmont Stakes — Damascus (Held at Aqueduct)

HORSE RACING

1962

- Australia - Melbourne Cup - Even Stevens
- Canada - Queen's Plate - Flaming Page
- France - Prix de l'Arc de Triomphe - Soltikoff
- Ireland - Irish Derby Stakes - Tambourine
- English Triple Crown Races:
    - Two Thousand Guineas Stakes - Privy Councillor
    - Epsom Derby - Larkspur
    - St. Leger Stakes - Hethersett
- United States Triple Crown Races:
    - Kentucky Derby - Decidedly
    - Preakness Stakes - Greek Money
    - Belmont Stakes - Jaipur

1963

- Australia - Melbourne Cup - Gatum Gatum
- Canada - Queen's Plate - Canebora
- France - Prix de l'Arc de Triomphe - Exbury
- Ireland - Irish Derby Stakes - Ragusa
- English Triple Crown Races:
    - Two Thousand Guineas Stakes - Only For Life
    - Epsom Derby - Relko
    - St. Leger Stakes - Ragusa
- United States Triple Crown Races:
    - Kentucky Derby - Chateaugay
    - Preakness Stakes - Candy Spots
    - Belmont Stakes - Chateaugay (Held at Aqueduct)

1964

- Australia - Melbourne Cup - Polo Prince
- Canada - Queen's Plate - Northern Dancer
- France - Prix de l'Arc de Triomphe - Prince Royal
- Ireland - Irish Derby Stakes - Santa Claus
- English Triple Crown Races:
    - Two Thousand Guineas Stakes - Baldric
    - Epsom Derby - Santa Claus
    - St. Leger Stakes - Indiana
- United States Triple Crown Races: Northern Dancer is the first Canadian-bred horse to win the Kentucky Derby
    - Kentucky Derby - Northern Dancer
    - Preakness Stakes - Northern Dancer
    - Belmont Stakes - Quadrangle (Held at Aqueduct)

HORSE RACING

1968

- Australia - Melbourne Cup - Royal Parma
- Canada - Queen's Plate - Merger
- France - Prix de l'Arc de Triomphe - Vaguely Noble
- Ireland - Irish Derby Stakes - Ribero
- English Triple Crown Races:
    - Two Thousand Guineas Stakes - Sir Ivor
    - Epsom Derby - Sir Ivor
    - St. Leger Stakes - Ribero
- United States Triple Crown Races:
    - Kentucky Derby - Forward Pass
    - Preakness Stakes - Forward Pass
    - Belmont Stakes - Stage Door Johnny

1969

- February 11 - Diana Crump becomes 1st American woman jockey to ride against men.
- February 22 - Barbara Jo Rubin wins a United States thoroughbred horse race making history as the first women to do so.
- Australia - Melbourne Cup - Rain Lover
- Canada - Queen's Plate - Jumpin Joseph
- France - Prix de l'Arc de Triomphe - Levmoss
- Ireland - Irish Derby Stakes - Prince Regent
- English Triple Crown Races:
    - Two Thousand Guineas Stakes - Right Tack
    - Epsom Derby - Blakeney
    - St. Leger Stakes - Intermezzo
- United States Triple Crown Races:
    - Kentucky Derby - Majestic Prince
    - Preakness Stakes - Majestic Prince
    - Belmont Stakes - Arts and Letters

1970

- Australia - Melbourne Cup - Baghdad Note
- Canada - Queen's Plate - Almoner
- France - Prix de l'Arc de Triomphe - Sassafrás
- Ireland - Irish Derby Stakes - Nijinsky II
- Nijinsky II wins the English Triple Crown Races:
    - Two Thousand Guineas Stakes - Nijinsky II
    - Epsom Derby - Nijinsky II
    - St. Leger Stakes - Nijinsky II
- United States Triple Crown Races:
    - Kentucky Derby - Dust Commander
    - Preakness Stakes - Personality
    - Belmont Stakes - High Echelon

HORSE RACING

1971

- Australia - Melbourne Cup - Silver Knight
- Canada - Queen's Plate - Kennedy Road
- France - Prix de l'Arc de Triomphe - Mill Reef
- Ireland - Irish Derby Stakes - Irish Ball
- English Triple Crown Races:
    - Two Thousand Guineas Stakes - Brigadier Gerard
    - Epsom Derby - Mill Reef
    - St. Leger Stakes - Athens Wood
- United States Triple Crown Races:
    - Kentucky Derby - Canonero II
    - Preakness Stakes - Canonero II
    - Belmont Stakes - Pass catcher

1972

- Australia - Melbourne Cup - Piping Lane
- Canada - Queen's Plate - Victoria Song
- France - Prix de l'Arc de Triomphe - San San
- Ireland - Irish Derby Stakes - Steel Pulse
- English Triple Crown Races:
    - Two Thousand Guineas Stakes - High Top
    - Epsom Derby - Roberto
    - St. Leger Stakes - Boucher
- United States Triple Crown Races:
    - Kentucky Derby - Riva Ridge
    - Preakness Stakes - Bee Bee Bee
    - Belmont Stakes - Riva Ridge

1973

- Australia - Melbourne Cup - Gala Supreme
- Canada - Queen's Plate - Royal Chocolate
- France - Prix de l'Arc de Triomphe - Rheingold
- Ireland - Irish Derby Stakes - Weaver's Hall
- English Triple Crown Races:
    - Two Thousand Guineas Stakes - Mon Fils
    - Epsom Derby - Morston
    - St. Leger Stakes - Peleid
- Secretariat, ridden by jockey Ron Turcotte, becomes the first horse in 25 years to win the United States Triple Crown Races:
    - Kentucky Derby - Secretariat
    - Preakness Stakes - Secretariat
    - Belmont Stakes - Secretariat

HORSE RACING

1974

- Australia - Melbourne Cup - Think Big
- Canada - Queen's Plate - Amber Herod
- France - Prix de l'Arc de Triomphe - Allez France
- Ireland - Irish Derby Stakes - English Prince
- English Triple Crown Races:
    - Two Thousand Guineas Stakes - Nonoalco
    - Epsom Derby - Snow Knight
    - St. Leger Stakes - Bustino
- United States Triple Crown Races:
    - Kentucky Derby - Cannonade
    - Preakness Stakes - Little Current
    - Belmont Stakes - Little Current

1975

- July 6 - In what was billed as the "Battle of the sexes," Kentucky Derby winner, Foolish Pleasure went head to head in a match race against the undefeated filly, Ruffian. In the lead, Ruffian broke a leg and after an unsuccessful operation to save her and was humanely put down.
- Australia - Melbourne Cup - Think Big
- Canada - Queen's Plate - L'Enjoleur
- France - Prix de l'Arc de Triomphe - Star Appeal
- Ireland - Irish Derby Stakes - Grundy
- English Triple Crown Races:
    - Two Thousand Guineas Stakes - Bolkonski
    - Epsom Derby - Grundy
    - St. Leger Stakes - Bruni
- United States Triple Crown Races:
    - Kentucky Derby - Foolish Pleasure
    - Preakness Stakes - Master Derby
    - Belmont Stakes - Avatar

1976

- Australia - Melbourne Cup - Van der Hum
- Canada - Queen's Plate - Norcliffe
- France - Prix de l'Arc de Triomphe - Ivanjica
- Ireland - Irish Derby Stakes - Malacate
- English Triple Crown Races:
    - Two Thousand Guineas Stakes - Wollow
    - Epsom Derby - Empery
    - St. Leger Stakes - Crow
- United States Triple Crown Races:
    - Kentucky Derby - Bold Forbes
    - Preakness Stakes - Elocutionist
    - Belmont Stakes - Bold Forbes

HORSE RACING

1977

- Australia - Melbourne Cup - Gold and Black
- Canada - Queen's Plate - Sound Reason
- France - Prix de l'Arc de Triomphe - Alleged
- Ireland - Irish Derby Stakes - The Minstrel
- English Triple Crown Races:
    - Two Thousand Guineas Stakes - Nebbiolo
    - Epsom Derby - The Minstrel
    - St. Leger Stakes - Dunfermline
- Seattle Slew, ridden by jockey Jean Cruguet, wins the United States Triple Crown Races:
    - Kentucky Derby - Seattle Slew
    - Preakness Stakes - Seattle Slew
    - Belmont Stakes - Seattle Slew

1978

- Australia - Melbourne Cup - Arwon
- Canada - Queen's Plate - Regal Embrace
- France - Prix de l'Arc de Triomphe - Alleged
- Ireland - Irish Derby Stakes - Shirley Heights
- English Triple Crown Races:
    - Two Thousand Guineas Stakes - Roland Gardens
    - Epsom Derby - Shirley Heights
    - St. Leger Stakes - Julio Mariner
- July 13: At Belmont Park, Elmont, New York, star jockey Ron Turcotte is injured in a racing accident that leaves him a paraplegic, ending his riding career.
- Affirmed, ridden by jockey Steve Cauthen, wins the United States Triple Crown Races by narrowly defeating Alydar in all three races:
    - Kentucky Derby - Affirmed, Alydar
    - Preakness Stakes - Affirmed, Alydar
    - Belmont Stakes - Affirmed, Alydar

1979

- Australia - Melbourne Cup - Hyperno
- Canada - Queen's Plate - Steady Growth
- France - Prix de l'Arc de Triomphe - Three Troikas
- Ireland - Irish Derby Stakes - Troy
- English Triple Crown Races:
    - Two Thousand Guineas Stakes - Tap On Wood
    - Epsom Derby - Troy
    - St. Leger Stakes - Son of Love
- United States Triple Crown Races:
    - Kentucky Derby - Spectacular Bid
    - Preakness Stakes - Spectacular Bid
    - Belmont Stakes - Coastal

HORSE RACING

1980

- Australia - Melbourne Cup - Beldale Ball
- Canada - Queen's Plate - Driving Home
- France - Prix de l'Arc de Triomphe - Detroit
- Ireland - Irish Derby Stakes - Tyrnavos
- English Triple Crown Races:
    - Two Thousand Guineas Stakes - Known Fact
    - Epsom Derby - Henbit
    - St. Leger Stakes - Light Cavalry
- United States Triple Crown Races:
    - Kentucky Derby - Genuine Risk
    - Preakness Stakes - Codex
    - Belmont Stakes - Temperance Hill

1981

- August 30 - John Henry becomes the first horse to win a million dollar race, the Inaugural Arlington Million, at Arlington Park in the Chicago suburb of Arlington Heights, Illinois.
- Australia - Melbourne Cup - Just a Dash
- Canada - Queen's Plate - Fiddle Dancer Boy
- France - Prix de l'Arc de Triomphe - Gold River
- Ireland - Irish Derby Stakes - Shergar
- English Triple Crown Races:
    - Two Thousand Guineas Stakes - To-Agori-Mou
    - Epsom Derby - Shergar
    - St. Leger Stakes - Cut Above
- United States Triple Crown Races:
    - Kentucky Derby - Pleasant Colony
    - Preakness Stakes - Pleasant Colony
    - Belmont Stakes - Summing

1982

- Australia - Melbourne Cup - Gurner's Lane
- Canada - Queen's Plate - Son of Briartic
- France - Prix de l'Arc de Triomphe - Akiyda
- Ireland - Irish Derby Stakes - Assert
- English Triple Crown Races:
    - Two Thousand Guineas Stakes - Zino
    - Epsom Derby - Golden Fleece
    - St. Leger Stakes - Touching Wood
- United States Triple Crown Races:
    - Kentucky Derby - Gato del Sol
    - Preakness Stakes - Aloma's Ruler
    - Belmont Stakes - Conquistador Cielo

HORSE RACING

1983

- February 8 - the great Shergar was kidnapped from Ballymany Stud, near the Curragh in County Kildare, Ireland. No trace of the horse has ever been found.
- Australia - Melbourne Cup - Kiwi
- Canada - Queen's Plate - Bompago
- France - Prix de l'Arc de Triomphe - All Along
- Ireland - Irish Derby Stakes - Shareef Dancer
- English Triple Crown Races:
    - Two Thousand Guineas Stakes - Lomond
    - Epsom Derby - Teenoso
    - St. Leger Stakes - Sun Princess
- United States Triple Crown Races:
- Sunny's Halo becomes on the second Canadian bred horse to win the Kentucky Derby.
    - Kentucky Derby - Sunny's Halo
    - Preakness Stakes - Deputed Testamony
    - Belmont Stakes - Caveat

1984

- Australia - Melbourne Cup - Black Knight
- Canada - Queen's Plate - Key to the Moon
- France - Prix de l'Arc de Triomphe - Sagace
- Ireland - Irish Derby Stakes - El Gran Senor
- English Triple Crown Races:
    - Two Thousand Guineas Stakes - El Gran Senor
    - Epsom Derby - Secreto
    - St. Leger Stakes - Commanche Run
- United States Triple Crown Races:
    - Kentucky Derby - Swale
    - Preakness Stakes - Gate Dancer
    - Belmont Stakes - Swale
- Breeders' Cup:
    - Breeders' Cup Classic - Wild Again
    - Breeders' Cup Distaff - Princess Rooney
    - Breeders' Cup Juvenile - Chief's Crown
    - Breeders' Cup Juvenile Fillies - Outstandingly
    - Breeders' Cup Mile - Royal Heroine
    - Breeders' Cup Sprint - Eillo
    - Breeders' Cup Turf - Lashkari

HORSE RACING

1985

- Australia - Melbourne Cup - What A Nuisance
- Canada - Queen's Plate - La Lorgnette
- France - Prix de l'Arc de Triomphe - Rainbow Quest
- Ireland - Irish Derby Stakes - Law Society
- English Triple Crown Races:
    - Two Thousand Guineas Stakes - Shadeed
    - Epsom Derby - Slip Anchor
    - St. Leger Stakes - Oh So Sharp
- United States Triple Crown Races:
    - Kentucky Derby - Spend a Buck
    - Preakness Stakes - Tank's Prospect
    - Belmont Stakes - Creme Fraiche
- Breeders' Cup:
    - Breeders' Cup Classic - Proud Truth
    - Breeders' Cup Distaff - Life's Magic
    - Breeders' Cup Juvenile - Tasso
    - Breeders' Cup Juvenile Fillies - Twilight Ridge
    - Breeders' Cup Mile - Cozzene
    - Breeders' Cup Sprint - Precisionist
    - Breeders' Cup Turf - Pebbles

1986

- Australia - Melbourne Cup - At Talaq
- Canada - Queen's Plate - Golden Choice
- France - Prix de l'Arc de Triomphe - Dancing Brave
- Ireland - Irish Derby Stakes - Shahrastani
- English Triple Crown Races:
    - Two Thousand Guineas Stakes - Dancing Brave
    - Epsom Derby - Shahrastani
    - St. Leger Stakes - Moon Madness
- United States Triple Crown Races:
    - Kentucky Derby - Ferdinand
    - Preakness Stakes - Snow Chief
    - Belmont Stakes - Danzig Connection
- Breeders' Cup:
    - Breeders' Cup Classic - Skywalker
    - Breeders' Cup Distaff - Lady's Secret
    - Breeders' Cup Juvenile - Capote
    - Breeders' Cup Juvenile Fillies - Brave Raj
    - Breeders' Cup Mile - Last Tycoon
    - Breeders' Cup Sprint - Smile
    - Breeders' Cup Turf - Manila

HORSE RACING

1987

- Australia - Melbourne Cup - Kensei
- Canada - Queen's Plate - Market Control
- France - Prix de l'Arc de Triomphe - Trempolino
- Ireland - Irish Derby Stakes - Sir Harry Lewis
- English Triple Crown Races:
    - Two Thousand Guineas Stakes - Don't Forget Me
    - Epsom Derby - Reference Point
    - St. Leger Stakes - Reference Point
- United States Triple Crown Races:
    - Kentucky Derby - Alysheba
    - Preakness Stakes - Alysheba
    - Belmont Stakes - Bet Twice
- Breeders' Cup:
    - Breeders' Cup Classic - Ferdinand
    - Breeders' Cup Distaff - Sacahuista
    - Breeders' Cup Juvenile - Success Express
    - Breeders' Cup Juvenile Fillies - Epitome
    - Breeders' Cup Mile - Miesque
    - Breeders' Cup Sprint - Very Subtle
    - Breeders' Cup Turf - Theatrical

1988

- Australia - Melbourne Cup - Empire Rose
- Canada - Queen's Plate - Regal Intention
- France - Prix de l'Arc de Triomphe - Tony Bin
- Ireland - Irish Derby Stakes - Kahyasi
- English Triple Crown Races:
    - Two Thousand Guineas Stakes - Doyoun
    - Epsom Derby - Kahyasi
    - St. Leger Stakes - Minister Son
- United States Triple Crown Races:
    - Kentucky Derby - Winning Colors
    - Preakness Stakes - Risen Star
    - Belmont Stakes - Risen Star
- Breeders' Cup:
    - Breeders' Cup Classic - Alysheba
    - Breeders' Cup Distaff - Personal Ensign
    - Breeders' Cup Juvenile - Is It True
    - Breeders' Cup Juvenile Fillies - Open Mind
    - Breeders' Cup Mile - Miesque
    - Breeders' Cup Sprint - Gulch
    - Breeders' Cup Turf - Great Communicator

HORSE RACING

1989

- Australia - Melbourne Cup - Tawrrific
- Canada - Queen's Plate - With Approval
- France - Prix de l'Arc de Triomphe - Carroll House
- Ireland - Irish Derby Stakes - Old Vic
- English Triple Crown Races:
    - Two Thousand Guineas Stakes - Nashwan
    - Epsom Derby - Nashwan
    - St. Leger Stakes - Michelozzo
- United States Triple Crown Races:
    - Kentucky Derby - Sunday Silence
    - Preakness Stakes - Sunday Silence
    - Belmont Stakes - Easy Goer
- Breeders' Cup:
    - Breeders' Cup Classic - Sunday Silence
    - Breeders' Cup Distaff - Bayakoa
    - Breeders' Cup Juvenile - Rhythm
    - Breeders' Cup Juvenile Fillies - Go for Wand
    - Breeders' Cup Mile - Steinlen
    - Breeders' Cup Sprint - Dancing Spree
    - Breeders' Cup Turf - Prized

1990

- Australia - Melbourne Cup - Kingston Rule
- Canada - Queen's Plate - Izvestia
- France - Prix de l'Arc de Triomphe - Saumarez
- Ireland - Irish Derby Stakes - Salsabil
- English Triple Crown Races:
    - Two Thousand Guineas Stakes - Tirol
    - Epsom Derby - Quest For Fame
    - St. Leger Stakes - Snurge
- United States Triple Crown Races:
    - Kentucky Derby - Unbridled
    - Preakness Stakes - Summer Squall
    - Belmont Stakes - Go and Go
- Breeders' Cup:
    - Breeders' Cup Classic - Unbridled
    - Breeders' Cup Distaff - Bayakoa
    - Breeders' Cup Juvenile - Fly So Free
    - Breeders' Cup Juvenile Fillies - Meadow Star
    - Breeders' Cup Mile - Royal Academy
    - Breeders' Cup Sprint - Safely Kept
    - Breeders' Cup Turf - In the Wings

HORSE RACING

1991

- Australia - Melbourne Cup - Let's Elope
- Canada - Queen's Plate - Dance Smartly
- France - Prix de l'Arc de Triomphe - Suave Dancer
- Ireland - Irish Derby Stakes - Generous
- English Triple Crown Races:
- Two Thousand Guineas Stakes - Mystiko Epsom Derby - Generous St. Leger Stakes - Toulon
- United States Triple Crown Races: Kentucky Derby - Strike the Gold Preakness Stakes - Hansel Belmont Stakes - Hansel
- Breeders' Cup:
- Breeders' Cup Classic - Black Tie Affair Breeders' Cup Distaff - Dance Smartly Breeders' Cup Juvenile - Arazi Breeders' Cup Juvenile Fillies - Pleasant Stage Breeders' Cup Mile - Opening Verse Breeders' Cup Sprint - Sheikh Albadou Breeders' Cup Turf - Miss Alleged

1992

- Pacer Artsplace voted "Harness Horse of the Year"
  - North America Cup - Safely Kept
- United States Pacing Triple Crown races:
  - Cane Pace - Western Hanover
  - Little Brown Jug - Fake Left
  - Messenger Stakes - Western Hanover
- United States Trotting Triple Crown races:
  - Hambletonian - Alf Palema
  - Yonkers Trot -
  - Kentucky Futurity - Annbro Keepsake
- Australian Inter Dominion Harness Racing Championship:
- Pacers: Westburn Grant
- Trotters: William Dee

1993

- Australia - Melbourne Cup - Vintage Crop Canada - Queen's Plate - Peteski France - Prix de l'Arc de Triomphe - Urban Sea Ireland - Irish Derby Stakes - Commander in Chief English Triple Crown Races: Two Thousand Guineas Stakes - Zafonic Epsom Derby - Commander in Chief St. Leger Stakes - Bob's Return
- United States Triple Crown Races:
  - Kentucky Derby - Sea Hero Preakness Stakes - Prairie Bayou Belmont Stakes - Colonial Affair Julie Krone, the all-time leading female jockey, became the first woman ever to win a Triple Crown race when she rode Colonial Affair to victory in the Belmont.
- Breeders' Cup:
  - Breeders' Cup Classic - Arcangues Breeders' Cup Distaff - Hollywood Wildcat Breeders' Cup Juvenile - Brocco Breeders' Cup Juvenile Fillies - Phone Chatter Breeders' Cup Mile - Lure Breeders' Cup Sprint - Cardmania Breeders' Cup Turf - Kotashaan

HORSE RACING

1994

- Australia - Melbourne Cup - Jeune Canada - Queen's Plate - Basquelan France - Prix de l'Arc de Triomphe - Carnegie Ireland - Irish Derby Stakes - Balanchine
- English Triple Crown Races:
    - Two Thousand Guineas Stakes - Mister Baileys Epsom Derby - Erhaab St. Leger Stakes - Moonax
- United States Triple Crown Races:
    - Kentucky Derby - Go for Gin Preakness Stakes - Tabasco Cat Belmont Stakes - Tabasco Cat
- Breeders' Cup:
    - Breeders' Cup Classic - Concern Breeders' Cup Distaff - One Dreamer Breeders' Cup Juvenile - Timber Country Breeders' Cup Juvenile Fillies - Flanders Breeders' Cup Mile - Barathea Breeders' Cup Sprint - Cherokee Run Breeders' Cup Turf - Tikkanen

1995

- Australia - Melbourne Cup - Doriemus Canada - Queen's Plate - Regal Discovery France - Prix de l'Arc de Triomphe - Lammtarra Ireland - Irish Derby Stakes - Winged Love
- English Triple Crown races:
    - Two Thousand Guineas Stakes - Pennekamp Epsom Derby - Lammtarra St. Leger Stakes - Classic Cliché
- United States Triple Crown races:
    - Kentucky Derby - Thunder Gulch Preakness Stakes - Timber Country Belmont Stakes - Thunder Gulch
- D. Wayne Lukas wins the Triple Crown, becoming the 12th trainer, and the first in history to win the Crown with different horses completing the sweep.
- Breeders' Cup:
    - Breeders' Cup Classic - Cigar Breeders' Cup Distaff - Inside Information Breeders' Cup Juvenile - Unbridled's Song Breeders' Cup Juvenile Fillies - My Flag Breeders' Cup Mile - Ridgewood Pearl Breeders' Cup Sprint - Desert Stormer Breeders' Cup Turf - Northern Spur

1996

- Australia - Melbourne Cup - Saintly Canada - Queen's Plate - Victor Cooley France - Prix de l'Arc de Triomphe - Helissio Ireland - Irish Derby Stakes - Zagreb
- English Triple Crown races: Two Thousand Guineas Stakes - Mark of Esteem Epsom Derby - Shaamit St. Leger Stakes - Shantou
- United States Triple Crown races: Kentucky Derby - Grindstone Preakness Stakes - Louis Quatorze Belmont Stakes - Editor's Note
- Breeders' Cup:
    - Breeders' Cup Classic - Alphabet Soup Breeders' Cup Distaff - Jewel Princess Breeders' Cup Juvenile - Boston Harbor Breeders' Cup Juvenile Fillies - Storm Song Breeders' Cup Mile - Da Hoss Breeders' Cup Sprint - Lit de Justice Breeders' Cup Turf - Pilsudski

HORSE RACING

1997

- Australia - Melbourne Cup - Might And Power Canada - Queen's Plate - Awesome Again France - Prix de l'Arc de Triomphe - Peintre Célèbre Ireland - Irish Derby Stakes - Desert King English Triple Crown races:
    - Two Thousand Guineas Stakes - Entrepreneur Epsom Derby - Benny the Dip St. Leger Stakes - Silver Patriarch
- United States Triple Crown races:
    - Kentucky Derby - Silver Charm Preakness Stakes - Silver Charm Belmont Stakes - Touch Gold
- Breeders' Cup:
    - Breeders' Cup Classic - Skip Away Breeders' Cup Distaff - Ajina Breeders' Cup Juvenile - Favorite Trick Breeders' Cup Juvenile Fillies - Countess Diana Breeders' Cup Mile - Spinning World Breeders' Cup Sprint - Elmhurst Breeders' Cup Turf - Chief Bearhart

1998

- Australia - Melbourne Cup - Jezabeel Canada - Queen's Plate - Archers Bay France - Prix de l'Arc de Triomphe - Sagamix Ireland - Irish Derby Stakes - Dream Well
- English Triple Crown races:
    - Two Thousand Guineas Stakes - King of Kings Epsom Derby - High Rise St. Leger Stakes - Nedawi
- United States Triple Crown races:
    - Kentucky Derby - Real Quiet Preakness Stakes - Real Quiet Belmont Stakes - Victory Gallop
- Breeders' Cup:
    - Breeders' Cup Classic - Awesome Again Breeders' Cup Distaff - Escena Breeders' Cup Juvenile - Answer Lively Breeders' Cup Juvenile Fillies - Silverbulletday Breeders' Cup Mile - Da Hoss Breeders' Cup Sprint - Reraise Breeders' Cup Turf - Buck's Boy

1999

- Australia - Melbourne Cup - Rogan Josh Canada - Queen's Plate - Woodcarver France - Prix de l'Arc de Triomphe - Montjeu Ireland - Irish Derby Stakes - Montjeu
- English Triple Crown races:
    - Two Thousand Guineas Stakes - Island Sands Epsom Derby - Oath St. Leger Stakes - Mutafaweq
- United States Triple Crown races:
    - Kentucky Derby - Charismatic Preakness Stakes - Charismatic Belmont Stakes - Lemon Drop Kid
- Breeders' Cup:
    - Breeders' Cup Classic - Cat Thief Breeders' Cup Distaff - Beautiful Pleasure Breeders' Cup Filly & Mare Turf - Soaring Softly Breeders' Cup Juvenile - Anees Breeders' Cup Juvenile Fillies - Cash Run Breeders' Cup Mile - Silic Breeders' Cup Sprint - Artax Breeders' Cup Turf - Daylami

HORSE RACING

2000

- Australia - Melbourne Cup - Brew
- Canada - Queen's Plate - Scatter the Gold
- France - Prix de l'Arc de Triomphe - Sinndar
- Ireland - Irish Derby Stakes - Sinndar
- English Triple Crown Races:
    - Two Thousand Guineas Stakes - Kings Best Epsom Derby - Sinndar St. Leger Stakes - Millenary
- United States Triple Crown Races:
    - Kentucky Derby - Fusaichi Pegasus Preakness Stakes - Red Bullet Belmont Stakes - Commendable
- Breeders' Cup:
    - Breeders' Cup Classic - Tiznow Breeders' Cup Distaff - Spain Breeders' Cup Filly & Mare Turf - Perfect Sting Breeders' Cup Juvenile - Macho Uno Breeders' Cup Juvenile Fillies - Caressing Breeders' Cup Mile - War Chant Breeders' Cup Sprint - Kona Gold Breeders' Cup Turf - Kalanisi

Lightning Source UK Ltd.
Milton Keynes UK
UKHW020633301220
376134UK00012B/1103